The

By the same author

Poetry

- Articulate Silences
- Cobwebs in the Sun
- Subterfuges
- Woodpeckers
- Trapfalls in the Sky
- Woolgathering

Novels

- The Bone's Prayer
- Nude Before God
- A River with Three Banks
- Infatuation

Short Stories

- Beyond Love and Other Stories

Play

- The Last Wedding Anniversary

Criticism

- Bergson and the Stream of Consciousness Novel

THE BEST OF FAIZ
(FAIZ AHMED FAIZ)

Translated
by
Shiv K Kumar

◫ UBSPD
UBS Publishers' Distributors Ltd.
New Delhi ● Bangalore ● Chennai
Calcutta ● Patna ● Kanpur ● London

UBS Publishers' Distributors Ltd.

5 Ansari Road, New Delhi-110 002
Phones: 3273601, 3266646 ● *Cable*: ALLBOOKS ● *Fax*: 3276593, 3274261
E-mail: ubspd@gobookshopping.com ● *Website*: www.gobookshopping.com
10 First Main Road, Gandhi Nagar, Bangalore-560 009
Phones: 2263901, 2263902, 2253903 ● *Cable*: ALLBOOKS ι
Fax: 2263904 ● *E-mail*: ubspd.bng@bgl.vsnl.net.in
6, Sivaganga Road, Nungambakkam, Chennai-600 034
Phones: 8276355, 8270189 ● *Cable* : UBSIPUB ι *Fax* : 8278920
E-mail: ubspd.che@md4.vsnl.net.in
8/1-B, Chowringhee Lane, Calcutta-700 016
Phones: 2441821, 2442910, 2449473 ● *Cable*: UBSIPUBS ι
Fax: 2450027 ● *E-mail*: ubspdcal@cal.vsnl.net.in
5 A, Rajendra Nagar, Patna-800 016
Phones: 672856, 673973, 686170 ● *Cable* : UBSPUB ● *Fax*: 686169
E-mail: ubspdpat@dte2.vsnl.net.in
80, Noronha Road, Cantonment, Kanpur-208 004
Phones: 369124, 362665, 357488 ● *Fax*: 315122
E-mail: ubsknp@lw1.vsnl.net.in

Distributors for Western India:
M/s Preface Books
Unit No. 223, (2nd floor), Cama Industrial Estate,
Sun Mill Compound, Lower Parel (W), Mumbai-400 013
Phones: 022-4988054 ● *Telefax*: 022-4988048 ● *E-mail: Preface @ vsnl.com*

Overseas Contact
475 North Circular Road, Neasden, London NW2 7QG, U.K.
Tele : (020) 8450-8667 ● *Fax* : (020) 8452 6612, *Attn*: UBS

© Shiv K Kumar

First Published **2001**

Shiv K Kumar asserts the moral right to be identified
as the translator of this work.

Cover Illustrator: Nand Katyal
Cover Design: Shamli Nimbalkar

Printed at Rajkamal Electric Press, New Delhi

For

Sharad Dutt —
One of the best things
that ever happened to me

Preface

Poet, journalist, translator, film-maker, broadcaster, Marxist activist and recipient of the Lenin Peace Prize, Faiz Ahmed Faiz grew into a legend in his life time. When he died on 20 November 1984, his admirers all over the world felt as though a literary era had come to an end.

I first met him in 1979 when he came to Hyderabad. I was asked to preside over one of his poetry readings. While introducing him to the audience, in what turned out to be my first ever public speech in Urdu, I said: 'Yé rahé Faiz Sahib - hum watan, hum zaban aur hum pésha...' This was because we were both natives of Lahore (a city he loved, although he was born in Sialkot); we shared the same mother tongue (Punjabi), and we had both started our careers as lecturers in English. But what I now cherish is the memory of an evening with him in Hyderabad. When I told him how his poetry had influenced mine, although I wrote in English, he responded modestly that he had been unjustifiably overrated, and that he was only too conscious of his limitations. There lay the secret of his charisma - that humility which is so rare in most contemporary writers. I then told him that while, as Professor of English, I lectured on British and American poetry, it was in his poetry, Iqbal's or Ghalib's, that I sought sustenance for my soul. To this he responded, with a dimpled smile: 'It's the mystique of words, I guess, that does it. Hasn't Urdu its unique aura of sound and meaning?... Also, an emotional charge of such high voltage as is not found in most western poetry.'

An irrepressible rebel, Faiz never submitted himself to anyform of tyranny - political, social or religious. As a poet-thinker, he believed that art should never be divorced from social reality. This commitment to social and political justice was accentuated by the long spells of incarceration he had to undergo. Prison, in fact, emerges in his poetry as a predominant metaphor that embodies his poetic vision.

Faiz was a patriot to the core of his being. His love for the motherland and his longing for the beloved often blend to soothe his mind and heart. One of his most moving poems, 'Do Ishq' ('Two Loves') is written on this theme: 'Just so have I craved for my other Laila, my Land/so has my heart fluttered with the same longing.'

His commitment to Marxism and his country's emancipation from oppression cannot be taken as the focal theme of his poetry. On the contrary, it is romantic love that often emerges as his supreme concern. Take, for instance, his poem 'Mauzu-e-Sukhan' ('Poesy's Domain') in which, while he recognises the validity of such themes as hunger and social injustice, he turns around to the muse's primal preoccupation – love.

These luscious corn fields bursting with youth -
why do they yield hunger alone?
All these themes are there indeed - and many more
but the gently parting lips of that beauty -
and, oh, the alluring contours of her body -
now tell me yourself, could there be such witchery
elsewhere?
Well, for me, this is it -
a poet's mental province can be none other than
this.

It would, therefore, be appropriate to say that Faiz's
all-embracing poetic vision is like a mighty river that
carries in its sweep countless tributaries. Faiz denies no
experience, excludes nothing to project reality in all its
baffling complexity. He is a poet of many moods, and
his work is a mosaic of diverse concerns - of classicism
and modernity, of political commitment and romantic
love, of affirmation and denial.

Faiz travelled widely abroad, often treating his
sojourns as spells of exile. Whether he was in Paris,
London, Moscow or Beirut, he always yearned for 'my
other Laila, my land.' This is how Edward Said, a
celebrated literary orientalist, describes his meeting with
Faiz:

'To see a poet in exile - as opposed to reading his
poetry of exile - is to see exile's antinomies embodied

and endured. Several years ago, I spent some time with Faiz Ahmed Faiz, the greatest of contemporary Urdu poets...'

Faiz was also widely read in western literature, particularly Latin American. So he could look at the western man from an oriental point of view, and the oriental from the western standpoint. It is this bifocal vision that lends a new dimension to his well-known poem 'Paris'. To him, the west is a wasteland of emotional sterility, of loneliness, of an innate incapacity for genuine emotion. To the western man, like Eliot's carbuncular lover, sex is a mere biological function.

The poetry of Faiz embodies the music of words. In a note on his boyhood and youth, he recalls how he was introduced to classical music by his friend Khwaja Khurshid Anwar, who was a member of the revolutionary group led by Bhagat Singh. This may explain Faiz's unique sense of rhythm, cadence, assonance and resonance. Of all the senses he evokes, the auditory is the most conspicuous. Even when his lines don't rhyme, as in his poem 'Yād' ('Remembrance'), any reader endowed with auditory imagination may 'hear' the reverbrations of the music that flows through it:

In the wilderness of my heart, O love,
waver
the shadows of your voice

the mirages of your lips ...
No wonder, his poetry lends itself so readily to ghazal singers like Iqbal Bano, Begum Akhtar, Mehdi Hasan and Nur Jehan. His language is multiversant; he can move effortlessly from formal prose syntax to free wheeling structures. After all, 'a poet,' he once remarked to a fellow Pakistani writer, 'is not a grammarian or a lexicographer. Language is his tool, the material he uses to create. It is thus subservient to him, not he to it.'

This brings me to another aspect of his poetry - is it classical or modern? While some critics consider him a traditionalist, others applaud him as an innovator. In fact, his poetry is a creative synthesis of both tradition and experiment. If he uses such traditional images as the caravan, the night of union or separation, the dawn of hope, etc., he never fails to alchemize each such image so as to invest it with a new meaning and coherence. In fact, his unique achievement, according to Edward Said, 'was to have created a contrapuntal rhetoric and rhythm whereby he could use classical forms (qasida, ghazal, musnavai) and transform them before his readers rather than break from the old forms ... The critical thing to understand about Faiz ... is that like Garcia Marquez he was read and listened to both by the literary élite and by the masses.'

If Faiz often refrained from responding to professional critics, it was because he believed that the poetic process was autotelic. In his introductory note to

Naqsh-e'-Faryadi, he wrote at the insistence of his publisher: 'So whenever these literary sleuths ask me why I write poetry, I often say anything that comes to my mind, just to put them off.' Only once did he open up to say that there was no fixed pattern in his mode of writing. Often while listening to music, a specific note or a certain rhythmic form would send him off to writing. Or it could be a line, a phrase or an image from a book he was reading ... Or, an exciting event, a sudden encounter with a stranger; in fact, anything anywhere could stir his imagination. While a ghazal, according to Faiz, emerges from a rhyming scheme in the poet's mind, a nazm demands deliberation.

It is difficult to sum up a poet whose multi-splendoured genius encompasses human experience in its entirety - mind, body and soul. I earnestly believe that, after Mir, Ghalib and Iqbal, he would be recognised as the greatest Urdu poet.

Shiv K Kumar.

In Memory of Faiz Ahmed Faiz

Your quest for release ---
the body's from the prison's padlock
the soul's from the body's dungeon.

How does it fare with you,
up there,
watching with Iqbal the unfettered falcons
of paradise, sailing across
the rivers of manna dew,
beds of myrrh and myrtle?

And how do the milk-bathed houris,
drunk on their scented youth,
thaw within your passion's hot clasp?

Since the Creator is no tyrant,
he can take a little censure sportingly--
even from his angels. Isn't an occasional
complaining the soul's prime sustenance?
So now you needn't dip your fingers
in your heart's blood, deprived of
your pen and paper.

In any case, all tyrants end up

in the other place

where the sun is noosed

in a nuclear freeze

the moon spits out venom

and the lakes burn like an oil tanker

Off the coast of Nigeria

Shiv K Kumar.

This poem was written on Faiz's first death anniversary, and published in the Siasat, Hyderabad.

Translator's Note

The Best of Faiz is an entirely new version of my earlier publication titled **Selected Poems of Faiz Ahmed Faiz** (Viking). It carries the Urdu text with parallel Roman script, a new introduction, several new poems - and substantive revisions, wherever necessary.

Translating Urdu poetry into English verse is a formidable task, especially when one undertakes to translate as difficult a poet as Faiz Ahmed Faiz, whose involuted thought processes often make his syntax very complex, almost intractable to rendition in a language whose diction, phrasing and rhytmic patterns are not tuned to oriental sensibuility. In fact, Faiz who was himself a very competent translator and who could handle both English and Urdu with great felicity, remarked:

"Translating poetry, even when confined to a cognate language with formal and idiomatic affinities with the original compositions, is an exacting task; but this task is obviously far more formidable when the languages involved are as far removed from each other in cultural background, rhythmic and formal patterns, and the vocabulary of symbol allusion as Urdu and English."

My task was, however, made easier by the generous help I received from such friends as Professors Taqi Ali Mirza, Syed Sirajuddin , Mr Ali Asghar and Dr. Yousuf Kamal. I may here mention that Dr. Yousuf Kamal has translated into Urdu my collection of poems, "Trapfalls in the Sky" (Macmillan) for the Sahitya Akademi (National Academy of Letters) with great sensitivity. This book has also been translated into Hindi, Tamil, Kannada and Malayalam - and published by the Sahitya Akademi.

Finally, I am indebted to Syed Ghulam Rabbani of The Munsif Daily who helped me with the Roman script -- and, specially, Mr. Muneeb Imran, Director of 'Dream Creations Multimedia Studio,' who undertook the arduous task of layout, typesettting, etc.

Shiv K Kumar

Contents

Dast-é-Tah-é-Sang

Sar-é Vadi's Sina

Shām-é Shaihr-é Yāran

Méré Dil Méré Musafir

Ghubār-é-Ayyām

Surod-é Shabana'h

سرودِ شبانہ

Nīm shab, chānd, <u>kh</u>ud faramoshi

نیم شب ، چاند ، خود فراموشی

maihfil-é-hast-o-bood veeran hai

محفلِ ہست و بود ویراں ہے

paikar-é iltija hai <u>kh</u>amoshi

پیکرِ التجا ہے خاموشی

bazm-é-anjum fasurda'h saman hai

بزمِ انجم فسردہ ساماں ہے

ābshār-é-sukoot jari hai

آبشارِ سکوت جاری ہے

char soo be<u>kh</u>udi si tāri hai

چار سوُ بے خودی سی طاری ہے

zindagi juzv-é-<u>kh</u>ab hai goya

زندگی جزوِ خواب ہے گویا

sari dunya sarāb hai goya

ساری دنیا سراب ہے گویا

so rahi hai ghané darakhton par

سوُ رہی ہے گھنے درختوں پر!

chandni ki thaki hu'ī āvāz

چاندنی کی تھکی ہوئی آواز

kahkashan nīm va ñigahon sé

کہکشاں نیم وا نگاہوں سے

kaih rahi hai ha<u>d</u>is-é-shauq-é-niyaz

کہہ رہی ہے حدیثِ شوقِ نیاز

sāz-é-dil ke <u>kh</u>amosh tāron sé

سازِ دل کے خموش تاروں سے

<u>ch</u>an raha hai <u>kh</u>umar-é-kaif agiñ

چھن رہا ہے خمارِ کیف آگیں

ārzoo, <u>kh</u>āb, téra roo-é-hasīñ

آرزوُ ، خواب ، تیرا رُوئے حسیں

1

The Melody of Night

Midnight, moon, self- forgetfulness—
desolate is the theatre of being.
Silence is desire incarnate
and sad the conclave of stars.
This ceaseless cataract of tranquillity--
oblivion reigns all around
as though existence is a mere fragment of a dream
and the entire world a mirage.

On the clustered treetops,
the jaded cry of moonlight sleeps.
With half-shut eyes, the constellations
seem to articulate my humble payer to you.
Through the mute heart-strings
filters the intoxication
that swells to ecstasy.

Desire, dream and your visage, so bewitching!

Teen Manzar

تین منظر

تصوُّر

Tasav'vūr

Shokhiyan muztar nigah-e-dida'h-e sarshar
mein
Ishratein khabīda'h rang-e-ghaza-e rukhsar
mein
surkh honton par tabassum ki ziyaein jis
tarah
yāsman ke phool doobe hon mai-e-gulnar
mein

شوخیاں مضطر نگاہ دیدۂ سرشار میں
عشرتیں خوابیدہ ہر نگہِ غازۂ رخسار میں
سرخ ہونٹوں پر تبسم کی ضیائیں جس طرح
یاسمن کے پھول ڈوبے ہوں مئے گلنار میں

Sāmna

سامنا

Chanti hu'i nazron se jazbat ki dunyaein
bekhābian, afsane, mahtab tamanna'ein
kuch uljhi hu'i bātein kuch baihke hu'e
naghme
kuch ashk jo ānkhon se be vajha chalak
ja'ein

چھنتی ہوئی نظروں سے جذبات کی دنیائیں
بے خوابیاں، افسانے، مہتاب، تمنائیں
کچھ الجھی ہوئی باتیں، کچھ بہکے ہوئے نغمے
کچھ اشک جو آنکھوں سے بے وجہ چھلک جائیں

Rukhsat

رخصت

Fasurdah rukh, labon par ek nīyaz amez
khamoshi
tabassum muzmahil tha marmarin haton
mein larzish thi
Voh kaisi bekasi thi teri purtamkin
nighahon mein
voh kya dukh tha teri saihmi hu'i khamosh
āhon mein

فسردہ رخ، لبوں پر اک نیاز آمیز خاموشی
تبسم مضمحل تھا، مرمریں ہاتھوں میں لرزش تھی
وہ کیسی بے کسی تھی تیری پُر تمکیں نگاہوں میں
وہ کیا دکھ تھا تیری سہمی ہوئی خاموش آہوں میں

Three Scences
Imagination

That playfulness, restless in her drunken eyes.

pleasures lurking in the talc's tints on her cheeks.

And on those crimson lips was her smile's glow

like jasmine dipped in the wine of flowers.

Encounter

A world of longing filtering through the eyes –

sleeplessness, tales, moon, yearnings.

Some tangled conversations, some stray strains -

and some tears in the eyes, for no reason.

Parting

Face woe-begone, on the lips silence tinged with humility,

the smile jaded and her marble hands aquiver.

What helplessness was there in your proud eyes

and what sorrow in your sighs, so mute and scared.

4

Donon jahān téri mohabbat mein hār
ké

Voh ja raha ko'i shab-é-gham guzar
ké

Virān hai maikada'h khum-o-saghar
udās hain

tum kya ga'é ké rooth ga'é din bahar
ké

Ek fursat-é-gunāh mili voh bhi chār
din

dekhé hain ham né hausalé
parvardigar ké

Dunya né téri yād sé begāna kar diya
tujh se bhi dilfaréb hain gham rozgar
ké

Bhoole se muskura t'o liyé thay voh
āj, Faiz

mat pooch valvalé dil-é- nakardahkar
ke

دونوں جہان تیری محبت میں ہار کے
وہ جارہا ہے کوئی شبِ غم گزار کے

ویراں ہے میکدہ، خم و ساغر اُداس ہیں
تم کیا گئے کہ رُوٹھ گئے دن بہار کے

اِک فرصتِ گناہ ملی، وہ بھی چار دن
دیکھے ہیں ہم نے حوصلے پروردگار کے

دنیا نے تیری یاد سے بیگانہ کر دیا
تجھ سے بھی دلفریب ہیں غم روزگار کے

بھولے سے مسکرا تو دیئے تھے وہ آج فیض
مت پوچھ ولولے دلِ ناکردہ کار کے

Losing both worlds ...

Losing both worlds in his love for you,

there goes someone, after a night of pain.

Desolate is the tavern, and despondent are

the cups and jars -

your parting has alienated me from the days of spring.

Four days was all the time I had for sinning ;

indeed, I've known the limits of God's bounty.

The world's grind has estranged me

from your remembrance -

the woes of life are more alluring than your love.

Unwittingly, as she broke into a smile today, O Faiz -

then ask me not how yearnings upsurged in this hapless

heart.

So'ch

سوچ

Kyoon dil méra shād nahin hai
kyoon khamosh raha karta hoon
choŗo méri rām kahani
main jaisa bhi hoon acha hoon
méra dil ghamgin hai to kya
ghamgin ye dunya hai sarī
Yé dukh téra hai na méra
ham sab ki jagīr hai pyari

کیوں میرا دل شاد نہیں ہے
کیوں خاموش رہا کر تا ہوں
چھوڑو میری رام کہانی
میں جیسا بھی ہوں اچھا ہوں
میرا دل غمگیں ہے تو کیا
غمگیں یہ دنیا ہے ساری
یہ دُکھ تیرا ہے نہ میرا
ہم سب کی جاگیر ہے پیاری

too gar méri bhi ho jā'e
dunya ké gham yōonhi rahéinge
pap ké phandé zulm ké bandhan
apné kahé sé kat na sakeingé

تو گر میری بھی ہو جائے
دنیا کے غم یوں ہی رہیں گے
پاپ کے پھندے ، ظلم کے بندھن
اپنے کہے سے کٹ نہ سکیں گے

gham har hālat mein mohlak hai
apna ho ya aur kisi ka
rona dhona jī ko jalana
yoon bhi hamara yoon bhi hamara

غم ہر حالت میں مہلک ہے
اپنا ہو یا اور کسی کا
رونا دھونا ، جی کو جلانا
یوں بھی ہمارا ، یوں بھی ہمارا

kyoon na jahan ka gham apnālein
bā'd mein sab tadbirein sochein
bā'd mein sukh ke sapne dekhéin
sapnon ki tadbirein sochein

کیوں نہ جہاں کا غم اپنالیں
بعد میں سب تدبیریں سوچیں
بعد میں سکھ کے سپنے دیکھیں
سپنوں کی تبیریں سوچیں

béfikre dhan daulat vālé
ye akhir kyoon khush rahte hain
In ka sukh āpas mein bāntein
ye bhi ākhir ham jaisé hain

بے فکرے دھن دولت والے
یہ آخر کیوں خوش رہتے ہیں
ان کا سکھ آپس میں بانٹیں
یہ بھی آخر ہم جیسے ہیں

ham né māna jang kaŗi hai
sar phooteingé khoon baihéga
khoon mein gham bhi baih ja'énge
ham na raheingé gham na rahéga

ہم نے مانا جنگ کڑی ہے
سر پھوٹیں گے ، خون بہے گا
خون میں غم بھی بہ جائیں گے
ہم نہ رہیں گے ، غم بھی نہ رہے گا

Reflections

Why is my heart so disconsolate?
Why am I always sunk in silence?
Leave me to my tale of woe
I'm happy as I am.

What if my heart is sorrowful,
sorrow looms over the entire world.
This pain is neither yours nor mine,
it's every human's inheritance, O love.

Even if you were mine, O love,
the world's sorrows will remain --
embroilment in sin and tyranny's hold -
could we just wish them all away?

Sorrow is lethal in every form,
be it mine or somebody else's.
Tears only singe the heart -
this way or that, pain will always remain.

Why not own up the world's suffering
and later ponder over the way out?
There'll then be time for dreaming
and unravelling the riddle of dreams.

Carefree are all the affluent -
why are they always cheerful ?
Let's share their joy and happiness,
for aren't they also like us ?

Indeed, the struggle would be relentless,
heads will be bashed and blood will flow:
Blood will wash away all pain –
and as we perish so will end our suffering.

رات یوں دل میں تری کھوئی ہوئی یاد آئی

جیسے ویرانے میں چپکے سے بہار آجائے

جیسے صحراوں میں ہولے سے چلے بادِ نسیم

جیسے بیمار کو بے وجہ قرار آجائے

دل رہین غم جہاں ہے آج

ہر نفس تشنہ فغاں ہے آج

سخت ویراں ہے محفلِ ہستی

اے غم دوست تو کہاں ہے آج

Rāt yoon dil mein téri khoi hu'i yād a'i

jaisé veerané mein chupké sé bahār āja'é

jaisé sahraon méin haulé śe chaſe ɓad-é-nasim

jaisé bimar ko bé-vajha qarār āja'é

dil rahin-é-gham-é-jahān hai āj

har nafas tishna-é-fughan hai aj

sakht yeerān hai maihfil-é-hasti

a'i gham-é-dost too kahān hai āj

Quatrains

Last night, a fugitive memory of you slid into my heart

as though a wilderness was quietly touched by

springtide,

as though some breeze came soughing through a

desert,

or someone sick, for no reason, felt reclaimed.

Today my heart feels indebted to the sorrows of this

world.

Each breath is famished for lament.

How profoundly desolate is all concourse of life---

O pain of love, where are you today?

حسینۂ خیال سے

مجھے دے دے

رسیلے ہونٹ، معصومانہ پیشانی، حسین آنکھیں

کہ میں ایک بار پھر رنگینیوں میں غرق ہو جاؤں

مری ہستی کو تیری اک نظر آغوش میں لے لے

ہمیشہ کے لئے اس دام میں محفوظ ہو جاؤں

ضیاءِ حسن سے ظلمات دنیا میں نہ پھر آؤں

گذشتہ حسرتوں کے داغ میرے دل سے دھل جائیں

میں آنے والی غم کی فکر سے آزاد ہو جاؤں

مرے ماضی و مستقبل سراسر محو ہو جائیں

مجھے وہ اک نظر، اک جاودانی سی نظر دے دے

Hasina-é-Khayal sé

Mujhé dé dé

Rasilé ho'nt, ma'soomana péshani, hasin ānkhéin
ke main ek bār phir ranginion mein gharq ho ja'ōn
meri hasti ko téri ek nazar āghosh mein lé lé
hamesha ké liyé i's dām mein mahfooz ho ja'on
Ziya-é-husn sé zulmat-é-dunya mein na phir a'on
guzishta hasraton ké dāgh méré dil sé dhul ja'éin
main āne vā'lé gham ki fikr sé azad ho ja'on
méré māzi o mustaqbil sarasar mahv hoja'ein
mujhé voh ek nazar, ek javedani si nazar dé dé

To My Love

Let me savour
      those sweet lips, that innocent forehead
      those beautiful eyes
      that I may once again drown myself in fantasy.

Let a glance of yours gather up
      my being into your lap
      so I may rest, secure in this trap
      never to return to life's darkness;
      all stains of my past yearnings may be
                  washed off,
      ridding me of the sable forebodings of the
                  future,
      sweeping away all my yesterdays and
                  tomorrows
      into oblivion.

Give me, my love, that one eternal glance----
      just once!

وقفِ حرمان و یاس رہتا ہے
دل ہے اکثر اداس رہتا ہے
تم تو غم دے کے بھول جاتے ہو
مجھ کو احساں کا پاس رہتا ہے

فضائے دل پہ اداسی بکھرتی جاتی ہے
فسردگی ہے کہ جاں تک اترتی جاتی ہے
فریب زیست سے قدرت کا مدعا معلوم
یہ ہوش ہے کہ جوانی گزرتی جاتی ہے

vaqf-é-hirmān-o-yās rahtạ hai

dil hai aksar udās rahta hai

tum t'o gham deké bhool jaté ho

mujh ko ehsāṅ ka pās rahta hai

faza-é-dil pé udāsi bikharti jāti hai

fasurdagi hai ké jān tak utarti jāti hai

faréb-é-zeest sé qudrat ka mudda'ā

    mā'loom

yé hosh hai ké javani guzarti jati hai

Given Away to Sorrow and Despair

Given away to sorrow and despair,

my heart often wilts away.

Your offering of pain, you forget

while I cherish what you have gifted me.

In the ambience of my heart, sorrow sprawls,

daspair seeps into my soul.

Life's illusion unfolds nature's intent--

all I'm conscious of is youth slipping away.

آج کی رات

آج کی رات ساز درد نہ چھیڑ

دکھ سے بھرپور دن تمام ہوئے

اور کل کی خبر کسے معلوم؟

دوش و فردا کی مٹ چکی ہیں حدود

ہو نہ ہو، اب سحر کسے معلوم؟

زندگی ہیچ! لیکن آج کی رات

ایذدیت ہے ممکن آج کی رات

آج کی رات ساز درد نہ چھیڑ

اب نہ دہر افسانہ ہائے الم

اپنی قسمت پہ سوگوار نہ ہو

فکرِ فردا اتار دے دل سے

عمرِ رفتہ پہ اشک بار نہ ہو

عہدِ غم کی حکایتیں مت پوچھ

ہو چکیں سب شکایتیں مت پوچھ

آج کی رات ساز درد نہ چھیڑ

Āj ki rāt

Āj ki rāt sāz-é-dard na cheṛ

dukh sé bharpoor din tamam hu'é

aur kal ki khabar kisé ma'loom?

dosh-o-farda ki mit chuki hain hudood

ho na ho ab sahar kise ma'loom?

zindagi hech! lékin āj ki rāt

ézadiyat hai mumkin āj ki rāt

āj ki rāt saz-é-dard na cheṛ

ab na dohra fasana'haé alam

apni qismat pé sogvar na ho

fikr-e-farda utār dé dil sé

umr-é-rafta pe ashkbār na ho

aih'd-é gham ki hikayatein mat pooch

ho chukin sab shikayatein mat pooch

  āj ki rāt saz-é-dard na cheṛ

Tonight

Don't thrum those chords of sorrow tonight--
gone is all my anguished past,
and who knows what tomorrow holds out.

The bounds of past and future blurred,
who knows if dawn will ever break.

Futile this dreary existence--but no,
it's possible to be a god tonight.

Don't thrum those chords of sorrow tonight,
recall those tales of gloom
or lament over your fate.

Don't let dread of the future haunt your mind,
nor shed tears over days gone by.

Don't now ask how things went awry,
for I'm done with all complaining.
So no more those tales of sorrow--

not tonight.

ایک منظر

بام و در خامشی کے بوجھ سے چور
آسمانوں سے جوئے درد رواں
چاند کا دکھ بھرا افسانہ نُور
شاہراہوں کی خاک میں غلطاں
خواب گاہوں میں نیم تاریکی
مضمحل لے رباب ہستی کی
ہلکے ہلکے سروں میں نوحہ کناں

Ek Manzar

Bām-o-dar khamushi ké bojh sé choor

āsmānon sé joo-é-dard ravan

chānd ka dukh bhara fasana-é-noor

shāhrāhon ki khāk mein ghaltān

khāb gahon mein nīm tārīki

muz'mahil lai rubāb-é-hasti ki

halké halké suron mein nauha kunān

A Scene

Terrace and door steeped in silence -

from the sky flows the river of desolation.

The moon's tragic tale of light

immersed in the dust of highways.

Semi-darkness in the chambers of night--and

the melody of life's lyre played out

in faint, elegiac strains.

میرے ندیم

Mére Nadīm

Khayal-o-shér ki dunya méin jān thi
     jin sé

faza-é-fikr-o-amal arghavan thi jin sé

voh jin ké noor sé shadab thay
     mah-o-anjum

junoon-é-ishq ki himmat javān thī jin
     sé

voh ārzooéin kahań so'gai hain méré
     nadīm?

voh nāsaboor nigahein, voh muntazir
     rahein

voh pās-é-zabt sé dil méin dabi hu'i
     āhein

voh intezar ki rātein, tavīl, tīra-o-tar

voh nīm khab shabistan, voh
     makhmalin bahein

kahaniyan thién, kahin kho ga'i hain,
     méré nadīm

machal raha hai rag-e-zindagi méin
     khoon-é-bahar

ulajh rahe hain purane ghamoń sé
     rooh ké tar

chalo ké chal ke charaghāń karein
     dayār-é-habīb

hain intézār mein agli mohabbatoń ké
     mazār

mohabbatéin jo fana ho ga'i hain

     méré nadīm!

خیال و شعر کی دنیا میں جان تھی جن سے

فضائے فکر و عمل ارغوان تھی جن سے

وہ جن کے نور سے شاداب تھے مہ و انجم

جنونِ عشق کی ہمت جوان تھی جن سے

وہ آرزوئیں کہاں سو گئی ہیں میرے ندیم؟

وہ ناصبور نگاہیں، وہ منتظر رہیں

وہ پاسِ ضبط سے دل میں دبی ہوئی آہیں

وہ انتظار کی راتیں، طویل تیرہ و تار

وہ نیم خواب شبستاں، وہ مخملیں باہیں

کہانیاں تھیں، کہیں کھو گئی ہیں، میرے ندیم

مچل رہا ہے رگِ زندگی میں خون بہار

الجھ رہے ہیں پرانے غموں سے روح کے تار

چلو کے چل کے چراغاں کریں دیارِ حبیب

ہیں انتظار میں اگلی محبتوں کے مزار

محبتیں جو فنا ہو گئی ہیں میرے ندیم!

My Friend

Those which were the soul of my fancy and verse,
lent their crimson to my thoughts, my deeds,
with whose effulgence glowed the moon and stars,
brought such courage to our love's frenzy--
where have those longings gone, my friend?

Those insatiate eyes, those waiting pathways,
those sighs in the heart for restraint
those nights of waiting, endless and dark--
those bedrooms, half-awake, those velvet arms--
mere yarns they were, where have they vanished,
                              my friend?

Sizzling in life's artery is spring's blood
the soul's strings entangled with past sorrows.
Let us go now and light up the house of the beloved
for lying in wait are the catacombs of past loves--
loves which have perished, my friend.

مجھ سے پہلی سی محبت مری محبوب نہ مانگ

Mujh se paih'li si mohabbat meri mahboob na mang

مجھ سے پہلی سی محبت مری محبوب نہ مانگ

میں نے سمجھا تھا کہ تو ہے تو درخشاں ہے حیات

تیرا غم ہے تو غم دہر کا جھگڑا کیا ہے

تیری صورت سے ہے عالم میں بہاروں کو ثبات

تیری آنکھوں کے سوا دنیا میں رکھا کیا ہے

تو جو مل جائے تو تقدیر نگوں ہو جائے

یوں نہ تھا، میں نے فقط چاہا تھا یوں ہو جائے

اور بھی دکھ ہیں زمانے میں محبت کے سوا

راحتیں اور بھی ہیں وصل کی راحت کے سوا

ان گنت صدیوں کے تاریک بہیمانہ طلسم

ریشم و اطلس و کمخواب میں بنوائے ہوئے

جا بجا بکتے ہوئے کوچہ و بازار میں جسم

خاک میں لتھڑے ہوئے خون میں نہلائے ہوئے

جسم نکلے ہوئے امراض کے تنوروں میں

پیپ بہتی ہوئی گلتے ہوئے ناسوروں میں

لوٹ جاتی ہے ادھر کو بھی نظر کیا کیجیے

اب بھی دلکش ہے ترا حسن مگر کیا کیجیے

اور بھی دکھ ہیں زمانے میں محبت کے سوا

راحتیں اور بھی ہیں وصل کی راحت کے سوا

مجھ سے پہلی سی محبت مری محبوب نہ مانگ

Mujh se paih'li si mohabbat meri
  mahboob na mang
main ne samjha tha ke too hai t'o
  darakshan hai hayat
tera gham hai to gham-e-daih'r ka jhagra
  kya hai
teri soorat se hai alam mein baharon ko
  sabat
teri ankhon ke siva dunya mein rakha
  kya hai
too jo mil ja'e to taqdir nigoon ho ja'e
yoon na tha, main ne faqat chaha tha
  yoon ho ja'e
aur bhi dukh hain zamane mein
  mohabbat ke siva
rahatein aur bhi hain vas'l ki rahat ke siva
anginat sadyon ke tarik bahimana'h tilism
resham-o-atlas-o-kimkhab mein bunva'e
  hu'e
ja baja bikte hu'e koocha o bazar mein
  jism
khak mein lithre hu'e khoon mein
  naihla'e hu'e
jism nikle hu'e amraz ke tannooron se
pip baihti hu'i galte hu'e nasooron mein
laut jati hai udhar ko bhi nazar kya kijey
ab bhi dilkash hai tera husn magar kya
  kijey
aur bhi dukh hain zamane mein
  mohabbat ke siva
rahatein aur bhi hain vas'l ki rahat ke siva
mujh se paih'li si mohabbat meri
  mahboob na mang

Ask Me Not for That Old Fervour

Ask me not for that old fervour, my love.
I had then imagined
     that your love would spark off my being,
     counterpoise the giant agony of the world--
     that your beauty would bring every spring to
          eternal blossom.
     And what else was there to cherish but
          your eyes?
     Once you were mine
     would not fate itself bow to me?
I had only willed it all
     but it was not to be,
     for there are sorrows other than heartache,
     joys other than love's rapture.
If there are spells of those dark, savage,
          countless centuriess--
     bodies robed in silk, satin and velvet--
     then aren't there also bodies
     traded down streets and alleyways--
     bodies smeared in dust, bathed in blood
     bodies emerging from ovens of sickness
     bodies with pus oozing from chronic sores?
If these images also seize my eye
     even though your beauty still enthrals,
     it's because there are sorrows other than
          heartache,
     joys other than love's rapture
So ask me not for that old fervour, my love.

Raqīb sé

Ā ké vabasta hain us husn ki yadéin
　　tujh sé
jis né is dil ko parikhana bana rakha
　　tha
jis ki ulfat méin bhula rakhi thi
　　dunya ham né
daihr ko daihr ka afsana bana rakha
　　tha
āshna hain téré qadmoṅ sé voh
　　rahein jin par
u's ki mad'hosh javani né inayat ki
　　hai
karvan guzré hain jin sé u'si ranā'i
　　ké
jis ki in ankhon né besood ibadat ki
　　hai
tujh sé kheli hain voh mahboob
　　havaéin jin méin
u's ké malboos ki afsurda'h mahék
　　baqi hai
tujh pé barsa hai usi bam se mahtab
　　ka noor
jis mein bīti hu'i rāton ki kasak baqi
　　hai
too né dékhi hai voh peshani, voh
　　rukhsār, voh ho'nt
zindagi jin ké tasavvur méin lutadi
　　ham né
tujh pe uthi hain voh khoi hu'i sahir
　　ankhein
tujh ko maloom hai kyoon umr
　　ganvadi ham né.
ham pé mushtar'ka hain, éhsan
　　gham-é ulfat ké
itne éhsan ké ginva'ooṅ to ginva na
　　sakooṅ
ham né is ishq mein kya khoya hai
　　kya paya hai
jūz téré aur ko samjhaooṅ to samjha
　　na sakooṅ

رقیب سے

آکر وابستہ ہیں اس حسن کی یادیں تجھ سے
جس نے اس دل کو پری خانہ بنار کھا تھا
جس کی الفت میں بھلا رکھی تھی دنیا ہم نے
دہر کو دہر کا افسانہ بنار کھا تھا
آشنا ہیں ترے قدموں سے وہ راہیں جن پر
اس کی مدہوش جوانی نے عنایت کی ہے
کارواں گزرے ہیں جن سے اسی رعنائی کے
جس کی ان آنکھوں نے بے سود عبادت کی ہے
تجھ سے کھیلی ہیں وہ محبوب ہوائیں جن میں
اس کے ملبوس کی افسردہ مہک باقی ہے
تجھ پر برساہے اسی بام سے مہتاب کا نور
جس میں بیتی ہوئی راتوں کی کسک باقی ہے
تونے دیکھی ہے وہ پیشانی، وہ رخسار، وہ ہونٹ
زندگی جن کے تصور میں لٹا دی ہم نے
تجھ پہ اٹھی ہیں وہ کھوئی ہوئی ساحر آنکھیں
تجھ کو معلوم ہے کیوں عمر گنوا دی ہم نے
ہم پہ مشترک ہیں احسان غم الفت کے
اتنے احسان کہ گنواوں تو گنوا نہ سکوں
ہم نے اس عشق میں کیا کھویا ہے کیا پایا ہے
جز ترے اور کو سمجھاؤں تو سمجھا نہ سکوں

To my Rival

O my rival, with you are associated my memories
of that face which made my heart a fairyland,
for whose love I'd forgotten this world,
letting its affairs sound like a yarn.

To your footfalls are known those pathways
along which her beauty has showered its gifts
along which have passed the caravans of her charm--
she, whom my eyes worshipped in vain.

With you have gambolled those love-laden winds
in which still lingers the sad fragrance of her dress.
On you has fallen, from her terrace,
that moonface's glow which still carries the pain of
                              past nights.

You have known that forehead, those cheeks, those lips
fantasizing which I've squandered away my life.
On you have risen those spellbinding eyes--
only you'd know why my life has been an endless
                              waste.

We have both shared the favours of love's sorrows--
far too many to count.
What we've learnt or lost in this affair,
I could explain to no one but you.

عاجزی سیکھی، غریبوں کی حمایت سیکھی
یاس و حرمان کے دکھ درد کے معنی سیکھے
زیر دستوں کے مصائب کو سمجھنا سیکھا
سرد آہوں کے رخ زرد کے معنی سیکھے
جب کہیں بیٹھ کے روتے ہیں وہ بیکس جن کے
اشک آنکھوں میں بلکتے ہوئے سو جاتے ہیں
ناتوانوں کے نوالوں پہ جھپٹتے ہیں عقاب
بازو تولے ہوئے، منڈلاتے ہوئے آتے ہیں
جب کبھی بکتا ہے بازار میں مزدور کا گوشت
شاہراہوں پہ غریبوں کا لہو بہتا ہے
آگ سی سینے میں رہ رہ کے ابلتی ہے نہ پوچھ
اپنے دل پر مجھے قابو ہی نہیں رہتا ہے

A'jizi sīkhi, gharibon ki himayat sīkhi
yas-o-hirman ke dukh dard ke ma'na
    sīkhe
zér daston ke masa'éb ko samajhna
    sīkha
sard āhon ke rukh-e zard ke ma'na
    sīkhe
jab kahin báith ke rote hain voh
    bekas jin ke
ashk ankhon mein bilakte hu'é so'jate
    hain
nā-to'ānon ke nivalon pé jhapaté hain
    uqāb
bā'zoo t'olé hu'é, mandlaté hu'é ā'té
    hain
jab kabhi bikta hai bazar mein
    mazdoor ka gosht
shahrahon pé gharibon ka la'hoo
    baihta hai.
Āg si siné mein rah rah ké ubalti hai
    na pooch
apné dil par mujhé qa'boo hi nahin
    rahta hai.

Humility I've learnt, sympathy for the poor,
learnt the meaning of despair, suffering and pain;
leant to comprehend the miseries of the oppressed,
the meaning of cold sighs, of pallid faces.

Whenever those hapless creatures sit together to cry,
in whose eyes tears, bitterly shed, fall asleep,
and those destitute upon whose morsels swoop down
the vultures hovering above, poised on their wing –

whenever is traded in the market place the flesh of the
                          labourer,
and on the highways flows theb lood of the poor,
a sort of fire upsurges in my bosom
and I lose all hold over my heart.

تنہائی

پھر کوئی آیا دلِ زار! نہیں، کوئی نہیں

راہرو ہوگا، کہیں اور چلا جائے گا

ڈھل چکی رات، بکھرنے لگا تاروں کا غبار

لڑکھڑانے لگے ایوانوں میں خوابیدہ چراغ

سو گئی راستہ تک تک کے ہر اک راہ گزار

اجنبی خاک نے دھندلا دیئے قدموں کے سراغ

گل کرو شمعیں بڑھادو مے و مینا و ایاغ

اپنے بے خواب کواڑوں کو مقفل کرلو

اب یہاں کوئی نہیں، کوئی نہیں آئے گا

Tanhā' i

Phir koi āya dil-e´zār! nahiṅ, koi nahiṅ

rāh-'rau hoga, kahin aur chalā jā'e´-ga

Dhal chuki rāt, bikharne´ laga taron ka ghubar

larkharane´ lage´ aivanoṅ mein khabida charagh

so'gaī rasta tak tak ke´ har ek rah-guzār

ajnabi khāk ne´ dhundla di'e´ qadmoṅ ke suragh

gul karo sham'e´in barhado mai'-o-mina-o-ayagh

apne be´-khab kivaroṅ ko muqaffal karlo

ab yahaṅ koi nahiṅ, koi nahiṅ a'-e´ga

27

Loneliness

Is someone out there again,
O my aggrieved heart?
No, perhaps some passerby, bound elsewhere.

The night is snapping at the seams,
scattered is the cluster of stars
and down the hallways
the drowsy tapers are gasping away.

Tired of the long wait,
every highway has fallen asleep,
every footprint blurred by the alien dust.

Put out the lights,
Put away the cups and wine--
and those doors which kept vigil all night,
lock them all.

Nobody will come here now --
No one!

راز الفت چھپا کے دیکھ لیا
دل بہت کچھ جلا کے دیکھ لیا

اور کیا دیکھنے کو باقی ہے
آپ سے دل لگا کے دیکھ لیا

وہ مرے ہو کے بھی مرے نہ ہوئے
ان کو اپنا بنا کے دیکھ لیا

آج ان کی نظر میں کچھ ہم نے
سب کی نظریں بچا کے دیکھ لیا

فیض تکمیل غم بھی ہو نہ سکی
عشق کو آزما کے دیکھ لیا

Rāz-e ulfat chupake´ dekh liya
dil bahut kuch jala ke´ dekh liya
aur kya dekhne´ ko bāqi hai
āp se´ dil laga ke´ dekh liya
voh mere´ ho'ke´ bhi mere´ na hu'-e´
un ko apna bana ke´ dekh liya
āj unki nazar mein kuch ham ne´
sab ki nazrein bacha ke´ dekh liya
Faiz takmīl-e gham bhi ho na saki
ishq ko āzma'ke´ dekh liya

I've Tried Camouflaging My Love's Secret

I've tried camouflaging my love's secret--
but even afflicting my heart was of no avail.

What else is there for me to know
after losing my heart to you?

She's mine, and yet not quite;
I've tried making her my own.

Today I saw in her eyes something
unnoticed by anyone around.

O Faiz, I'd longed for sorrow's fruition,
but not even love could do it for me.

پھر حریفِ بہار ہو بیٹھے

جانے کس کس کو آج رو بیٹھے

تھی، مگر اتنی رائگاں بھی نہ تھی

آج کچھ زندگی سے کھو بیٹھے

تیرے در تک پہنچ کے لوٹ آئے

عشق کی آبرو ڈبو بیٹھے

ساری دنیا سے دور ہو جائے

جو ذرا تیرے پاس ہو بیٹھے

نہ گئی تیری بے رخی نہ گئی

ہم تری آرزو بھی کھو بیٹھے

فیض ہو تا رہے جو ہونا ہے

شعر لکھتے رہا کرو بیٹھے

Phir harif-é bahar ho bai'thé

ja'né kis kis ko āj ro' baithé

thi, magar itni ra'égān bhi na thi

āj kuch zindagi sé kho bai'thé

téré dar tak pahunch ké laut ā'é

ishq ki ābroo dubo bai'théy

sari dunya sé door ho'jā é

jo zara téré pās ho bai'thé

na ga'ī teri bé-rukhi na ga'ī

ham téri arzoo bhi kho bai'thé

Faiz hota rahe jo hona hai

shér likhté raha karo baithéy

Again, I Am a Rival of Spring

Again, I am a rival of spring--
such is my sorrow today over friends lost.

Futile was life, but not so much--
today something seems to have faded out of my life.

Making it to your doorstep and then returning--
wasn't that tainting the fair name of love?

One moves away from the entire world
when one sits close beside you.

Never did you give up your indifference,
even though I've forsaken all yearning for you.

O Faiz, let things take their own course--
you'd better keep spinning out your verses.

Chand ro'z aur meri jān!

Chand ro'z aur meri jān faqat
    chand hi ro'z
zulm ki chaon mein dam lene
    pe majboor hain ham
aur kuch der sitam saih' lein,
    tarap lein, ro' lein
apne ajdād ki mīras hai ma'zoor
    hain ham

jism par qaid hai, jazbat pe
    zanjirein hain
fikr mahboos hai, guftar pe
    tazirein hain
apni himmat hai ke ham phir
    bhi jiye jāte hain
zindagi kya kisi muflis ki qaba
    hai jis mein
har ghari dard ke paivand lage
    jā'te hain
lekin ab zulm ki mi'ād ke din
    thore hain
ek zara sabr ke faryad ke din
    thore hain

arsa-é-daihr ki jhulsi hu'i virāni
    mein
ham ko rahna hai, pe yoonhi to
    nahin rahna hai
ajnabi haton ka be'nam giranbar
    sitam
āj saihna hai hamesha to nahin
    saihna hai
ye tere husn se lipti hu'i ālām ki
    gard
apni do'roza'h javani ki
    shikaston ka shumar
chāndni rāton ka bekar daihekta
    hu'a dard
dil ki be'sood tarap, jism ki
    mayoos pukār
chand ro'z aur meri jan faqat
chand hi ro'z.

چند روز اور مری جان!

چند روز اور مری جان فقط چند ہی روز
ظلم کی چھاؤں میں دم لینے پہ مجبور ہیں ہم
اور کچھ دیر ستم سہ لیں، تڑپ لیں، رو لیں
اپنے اجداد کی میراث ہے معذور ہیں ہم

جسم پر قید ہے، جذبات پہ زنجیریں ہیں
فکر محبوس ہے، گفتار پہ تعذیریں ہیں
اپنی ہمت ہے کہ ہم پھر بھی جئے جاتے ہیں
زندگی کیا کسی مفلس کی قبا ہے جس میں
ہر گھڑی درد کے پیوند لگے جاتے ہیں
لیکن اب ظلم کی میعاد کے دن تھوڑے ہیں
اک ذرا صبر کہ فریاد کے دن تھوڑے ہیں

عرصۂ دہر کی جھلسی ہوئی ویرانی میں
ہم کو رہنا ہے، پہ یونہی تو نہیں رہنا ہے
اجنبی ہاتھوں کا بے نام گرانبار ستم
آج سہنا ہے، ہمیشہ تو نہیں سہنا ہے
یہ ترے حسن سے لپٹی ہوئی آلام کی گرد
اپنی دو روزہ جوانی کی شکستوں کا شمار
چاندنی راتوں کا بے کار دہکتا ہوا درد
دل کی بے سود تڑپ، جسم کی مایوس پکار
چند روز اور مری جان فقط چند ہی روز

33

A Few Days More, My Love

A few days more, my love, just a few days--
are we fated to live in tyranny's shadow.
Let us endure a little longer --
oppression, writhing and tears.

All this is our legacy; we are helpless.
Body imprisioned, emotions shackled,
thought chained and speech censored.
It's just our courage that keeps us going.
Life is a beggar's tunic that picks on
patches of pain each moment.
But now the days of tyranny are numbered.
Just a little patience,
since the days of entreaty are nearly done.

In this scorched wasteland of life,
we're destined to live, but not like this.
This nameless, heavy oppression of alien hands,
we may have to endure today, but not forever.
This dust of torments smearing your beauty--
this dwelling on frustrations of our passing youth,
this futile, throbbing pain of moonlit nights,
this vain writhing of the heart, the body's helpless cry--
a few days more, my love, just a few days!

Kut'té

كتّے

Ye galyon ké avara'h békar kut'té
ké bakhsha gaya jin ko zauq-é-gadā'i
zamané ki phitkar sarma'yah unka
jahān bhar ki dhutkar unki kama'ī
na āram shab ko na rāhat savéré
ghilazat mein ghar, naliyon mein baséré
jo bigrein to ek doosré sé lara'do
zara ék roti ka tukra dikha'do
yé har ék ki thokarein khané' vā'lé
yé fāqon sé ukta ké marjané vālé

yé mazloom makhlooq gar sar utha'é
t'o insan sab sarkashi bhool ja'é
yé chāhéin to dunya ko apna banaléin
yé aqa'on ki haddiyan tak chabaléin
ko'i in'ko éhsas-é zillat dila dé
koi in'ki so'i hu'i dum hila dé

Dogs

Tramping about the streets aimlessly, these dogs,
born to the prerogative of beggary--
their only treasure is the world's scorn
their only wages, the world's reproof.

Not a moment's respite, day or night--
dirt their abode, drains their rest-houses.

If roused, they may be set one against the other,
just dangle before them a morsel of bread--
they who suffer everybody's kicks,
who'd tire and die of starvation.

If these destitutes were ever stirred up,
man would forget his imperiousness.
If only they willed, they'd reign supreme
for they could chew up even the bones of their
                                        masters.

All this--
if only someone would awaken them to their ignominy,
shake their sagging tails
to action!

بول

بول کہ لب آزاد ہیں تیرے

بول، زباں اب تک تیری ہے

تیرا ستواں جسم ہے تیرا

بول کہ جاں اب تک تیری ہے

دیکھ آہنگر کی دکاں میں

تند ہیں شعلے، سرخ ہے آہن

کھلنے لگے قفلوں کے دہانے

پھیلا ہر اک زنجیر کا دامن

بول، یہ تھوڑا وقت بہت ہے

جسم و زباں کی موت سے پہلے

بول، کہ سچ زندہ ہے اب تک

بول، جو کچھ کہنا ہے کہہ لے!

Bo'l

Bo'l ké lab azad hain téré

bo'l, zaban ab tak téri hai

téra sutvāṅ jism hai téra

bo'l ké jāṅ ab tak téri hai

dékh āhangar ki dūkaṅ mein

ṭund hain sho'lé, surkh hai āhan

khulné lagé quflon ké dahāné

phaila har ek zanjīr ka dāman

bo'l, ye thoṛa vaqt bahut hai

jism-o-zabaṅ ki maut sé paih'lé

bo'l, ké sach zinda hai ab tak

bo'l, jo kuch kaih'na hai kaih lé!

Speak Up!

Speak up, for your lips are not sealed
and your words are still your own.
This upright body is yours –
speak, while your soul is still your own.

Look there, in that smithy,
its red oven, fierce flames,
the padlocks are already opening their mouths
and each fetter is skirting around.

Speak up now, for time's running out.
Before your body and mind fade away,
tell us, for truth is not yet dead.

Speak
whatever you have to say!

موضوعِ سخن

Mauzoo-e Sukhan

گل ہوئی جاتی ہے افسردہ سلگتی ہوئی شام

دھل کے نکلے گی ابھی چشمہ مہتاب سے رات

اور۔۔۔ مشتاق نگاہوں کی سنی جائے گی

اور۔۔۔ان کے ہاتھوں سے مس ہوں گے یہ ترسے ہوئے ہاتھ

Gul hu'i ja'ti hai afsurda'h sulagti hu'i sham

dhul ke nikle'gi abhi chashma-e mahtab se rat

aur--- mushtaq nigahon ki suni ja'e gi

aur--- un ke hathon se mas hon'ge yeh tarse hu e haath

ان کا آنچل ہے کہ رخسار کہ پیراہن ہے

کچھ تو ہے جس سے ہوئی جاتی ہے چلمن رنگیں

u'n ka anchal hai ke rukhsar ke pairahan hai

kuch to hai jis se hu'i ja'ti hai chilman rangin

جانے اس زلف کی موہوم گھنی چھاوں میں

ٹمٹماتا ہے وہ آویزہ ابھی تک کہ نہیں

Ja'ne u's zulf ki mauhoom ghani cha'on mein

timtimata hai voh a 'vezah abhi tak ke nahin

آج پھر حسنِ دل آرا کی وہی دھج ہو گی

وہی خوابیدہ سی آنکھیں وہی کاجل کی لکیر

رنگِ رخسار پہ ہلکا سا وہ غازے کا غبار

صندلی ہاتھ پہ دھندلی سی حنا کی تحریر

aj phir husn-e dil'ara ki vohi dhaj hogi

vohi khabida si ankhein vohi kajal ki lakir

rang-e rukhsar pe halka sa voh gha'ze ka ghubar

sandali hath pe dhundli si hina ki tahrir

اپنے افکار کی،اشعار کی دنیا ہے یہی

جان مضموں ہے یہی شاہد معنی ہے یہی

آج تک سرخ و سیہ صدیوں کے سائے کے تلے

آدم و حوا کی اولاد پہ کیا گزری ہے

موت اور زیست کی روزانہ صف آرائی میں

ہم پہ کیا گزری ہے اجداد پہ کیا گزری ہے؟

apne afkar ki, ash'ar ki dunya hai yehi

jan-e mazmon hai yehi shahid-e ma'na hai yehi

aj tak surkh-o-siyah sadyon ke sa'ye ke ta'le

Adam-o-havva ki aulad pe kya guzri hai

Maut aur zist ki roz'ana saf'arai mein

Ham pe kya guzri hai ajdad pe kya guzri hai?

Poesy's Domain

This evening, forlorn--its embers smouldering.
Out of the moon's spring will emerge night, cleansed--
and my eager eyes will be rewarded
as my impatient hands touch yours.

Is it her stole, her cheeks or her dress--
something surely lends the screen such colour.
I wonder if in the deep, faint shadow of your locks
there still glimmers that eardrop.

Today again, there'll be the same splendour
of that bewitching beauty,
the same drowsy eyes, the same streak of collyrium
on her cheek the mellowed tint of talc,
on her sandalwood palms a blurred line of henna.

This alone is the domain of my thoughts--
my verse, its sole quintessence.

Till today, in the shadow of centuries, sanguine
                                    and sable,
what has been the lot of Adam's progeny?
In the daily battle-array of death and life,
how will it fare with us, how had it fared with
                            our ancestors?

In daihekté hu'é shaihron ki
    faravan makhlooq
kyoon faqat marné ki hasrat
    mein jiya karti hai?

یہ دیکھتے ہوئے شہروں کی فراواں مخلوق
کیوں فقط مرنے کی حسرت میں جیا کرتی ہے؟

ye hasin khét phata parta hai
    joban jin ka
kis liyé in méin faqat bhook
    uga karti hai

یہ حسیں کھیت پھٹا پڑتا ہے جو بن جن کا
کس لئے ان میں فقط بھوک اگا کرتی ہے

ye har ék simt pur'asrar kari
    dīvarein
Jal bujhé jin méin hazaron ki
    javani ké charagh
ye har ék gām pé in khabon ki
    maqtal' gahéin
jin ké partau sé charaghan hain
    hazaron ké damagh

یہ ہر اک سمت پر اسرار کڑی دیواریں
جل بجھے جن میں ہزاروں کی جوانی کے چراغ
یہ ہر اک گام پہ ان خوابوں کی مقتل گاہیں
جن کے پر تو سے چراغاں ہیں ہزاروں کے دماغ

ye bhi hain aisé kai aur bhi
    mazmoon hon'gé
Lékin u's shokh ké ā'hista sé
    khulté hu'é ho'nt
Hā'é u's jism ké kambakht
    dil'āvez khutoot
Āp hi kahiyé kahin aisé bhi
    afsoon hon'gé

یہ بھی ہیں ایسے کئی اور بھی مضمون ہوں گے
لیکن اس شوخ کے آہستہ سے کھلتے ہوئے ہونٹ
ہائے اس جسم کے کم بخت دل آویز خطوط
آپ ہی کہئے کہیں ایسے بھی افسوں ہوں گے

Apna mauzoo-é sukhan in'ké
    siva aur nahiň
Tab-é shā'ir ka vatan in'ké siva
    aur nahiň

اپنا موضوع سخن ان کے سوا اور نہیں
طبع شاعر کا وطن ان کے سوا اور نہیں

The jostling crowds of these glittering cities--
why do they sustain themselves on a mere death-wish?
These luscious corn-fields bursting with youth--
why do they yield hunger alone?

These impregnable, mysterious walls all around,
                          within which
were snuffed out the lamps of countless young
                          hearts.
At every step, these abattoirs of dreams
whose reflections have ignited the minds of multitudes.

All these themes are there indeed--and many more;
but the gently parting lips of that beauty--
and oh, the alluring contours of her body--
now tell me yourself, could there be such
                              witchery elsewhere?

Well, for me this is it--
a poet's mental province can be none other than this.

هم لوگ

Ham Lo'g

Dilke ai'van mein liyé gul-shudah
    sham'on ki qatar
noor-é khurshid sé saihme hu'é
    ukta'é hu'é
husn'é mahboob ké sayyal
    tasavvur ki tar'h
apni tariki ko bhīnche hu'é
    lipta'é-hu'é

ghayat'é sood-o-zian, soorat'é
    aghāz-o-ma'al
vohi bé'sood tajassus, vohi bekar
    sawal
muz'mahil sa'at-é imroz ki
    bé'rangi sé
yād-é-mazi sé ghamin, daihshat-é
    farda sé nidhal
tish'nah afkar jo taskin nahin pā'té
    hain
sokhta'h ashk jo ankhon méin
    nahin ā'té hain
ek kara dard ké jo gīt mein dhalta
    hi nahin
dil ke tarīk shigafon sé nikalta hi
    nahin
aur ék uljhi hu'i mauhoom si
    darmān ki talash
dasht-o-zindan ki havas, chak'é
    giréban ki talash

دل کے ایوان میں لئے گل شدہ شمعوں کی قطار
نور خورشید سے سہمے ہوئے اکتائے ہوئے
حسن محبوب کے سیال تصور کی طرح
اپنی تاریکی کو بھینچے ہوئے لپٹائے ہوئے

غایت سود و زیاں، صورت آغاز و مال
وہی بے سود تجسس، وہی بے کار سوال
مضمحل ساعت امروز کی بے رنگی سے
یاد ماضی سے غمیں، دہشت فردا سے نڈھال
تشنہ افکار جو تسکین نہیں پاتے ہیں
سوختہ اشک جو آنکھوں میں نہیں آتے ہیں
اک کڑا درد کہ جو گیت میں ڈھلتا ہی نہیں
دل کے تاریک شگافوں سے نکلتا ہی نہیں
اور اک الجھی ہوئی موہوم سی درماں کی تلاش
دشت و زنداں کی ہوس چاک گریباں کی تلاش

We People

Carrying in the hallways of our hearts
rows of extinguished lamps
bored and fearful of sunlight
like the mercurial image of the beloved's beauty,
hugging our darkness, wrapped up in it.

Our concern – loss and gain
beginning and end--
the same futile curiosity, the same pointless quest.
Fatigued by the greyness of the daily scene,
grieving over the remembrance of things past,
enervated by the dread of the future.

Unquenched thoughts, never satiated;
burnt-out tears that never well up in the eyes--
a harsh pain that never melts into a song,
never oozes from the heart's dark crevices.
And a quest, confused, ethereal, for some panacea,
a craving for the wilderness and the prison,
a quest for the ripped collar.

شاہراہ

ایک افسردہ شاہراہ ہے دراز
دور افق پر نظر جمائے ہوئے
سرد مٹی پہ اپنے سینے کے
سرمگیں حسن کو بچھائے ہوئے

جس طرح کوئی غمزدہ عورت
اپنے ویراں کدے میں محو خیال
وصل محبوب کے تصور میں
مو بمو چور، عضو عضو نڈھال

Shāh'rāh

Ek afsurda shāh'rāh'e daraz
dōor ufaq par nazar jama'e' hu'e'
sard mitti pe' apne' si'ne' ke'
surmagin husn ko bichāye' hu'e'

jis tar'h koi gham'zadah au'rat
apne' vīran'kade' mein mahv'e' khayal
vasl'e' mahboob ke' tasavvur me'in
moo ba-moo choor, az'v az'v nidhāl

Highway

A sad highway, stretching endlessly--
its eyes riveted on the remote horizon.
The cold earth of its bosom
overspread with its grey beauty,

as though some woman grieving
in her desolate home,
immersed in thoughts
of union with her beloved--
each pore, each limb
limp with desire.

متاعِ لوح و قلم چھن گئی تو کیا غم ہے!
کہ خونِ دل میں ڈبو لی ہیں انگلیاں میں نے
زباں پہ مہر لگی ہے تو کیا کہ رکھ دی ہے!
ہر اک حلقۂ زنجیر میں زباں میں نے

Matae' lauh-o-qalam chin gai t'o kya gham hai!

ke khoon-e' dil mein dubo'li hain ungliyan main ne'

zuban pe' moh'r lagi hai to kya ke rakh' di hai!

har ek halqa-e zanjir mein zuban main ne'

تراجمال نگاہوں میں لے کے اٹھا ہوں
نکھر گئی ہے فضا تیرے پیرہن کی سی
نسیم تیرے شبستاں سے ہو کے آئی ہے
مری سحر میں مہک ہے ترے بدن کی سی

Tera jamal nigahon mein le'ke' utha hoon

nikhar'ga'i hai faza tere pairahan ki si

nasim tere shabistan se' ho'ke' ā'ī hai

meri sahar mein mai'hak hai tere' badan ki si

47

Quatrains

What if my pen and paper have been snatched away,
I've dipped my fingers in the heart's blood,
What if my lips are sealed,
I've lent my tongue to each link in the chain.

Eyes drunk on your beauty, I rise--
the air feels spruced up like your robe.
The breeze must have wafted through your
                                    bed-chamber,
so redolent of your body is my dawn.

اے دل بیتاب ٹھہر!

Ai dil'-é bétab thaih'r

تیزگی ہے کہ امڈتی ہی چلی آتی ہے

Tiragi hai ké umadti hi chali āti hai

شب کی رگ رگ سے لہو پھوٹ رہا ہو جیسے

shab ki rag rag sé lahoo phoot raha
    ho jaise

چل رہی ہے کچھ اس انداز سے نبض ہستی

chal rahi hai ku<u>ch</u> is andāz sé nabz-é
    hasti

دونوں عالم کا نشہ ٹوٹ رہا ہو جیسے

dono'n ālam ka nisha'h toot raha ho
    jaisé

رات کا گرم لہو اور بھی بہہ جانے دو

rāt ka gar'm lahoo aur bhi baih ja'né
    do

یہی تاریکی تو ہے غازہ رُخ خسار سحر

yehi tariki to hai ghaza-é rukhsar'é
    sahar

صبح ہونے ہی کو ہے اے دل بیتاب ٹھہر

sub'h honé hi ko hai ai dil-e betab
    thaihr

ابھی زنجیر چھنکتی ہے پس پردہ ساز

abhi zanjir <u>ch</u>anakti hai pa's-e
    pardah-é saz

مطلق الحکم ہے شیر ازۂ اسباب ابھی

mutlaqul hukm hai shiraza-é asbab
    abhi

ساغرِ ناب میں آنسو بھی ڈھلک جاتے ہیں

saghar'e nāb méin ansoo bhi dhalak
    ja'té hain

لغزش پا میں ہے پابندی آداب ابھی

laghzish-e pā méin hai pabandi-é
    ādab abhi

اپنے دیوانوں کو دیوانہ تو بن لینے دو

apne divanon ko divana t'o ban léné
    d'o

اپنے مے خانوں کو میخانہ تو بن لینے دو

apné maikhanon ko mai'khana to
    ban lené d'o

جلد یہ سطوت اسباب بھی اٹھ جائے گی

jald yé satvat-é asbab bhi u<u>th</u> ja'égi

یہ گرانباری آداب بھی اٹھ جاء گی

yé giranbari-é adāb bhi uth ja'égi

خواہ زنجیر چھنکتی رہے، چھنکتی ہی رہے

<u>kh</u>āh zanjir <u>ch</u>anakti rahé, <u>ch</u>anakti
    hi rahé.

Hold On, Restless Heart

Darkness that's billowing up –
as though from every vein of the night, blood
gushes forth.
The pulse of life throbs
as the intoxication of both worlds fades away.

Hot blood of the night,
let it gush forth still more –   after all,
this very darkness powders the dawn's cheeks.
It will soon be day--hold on, restless heart.

The chains still clank behind the screen of music,
the package of goods and chattel still holds its
inexorable sway.
In the red wine, even the tears get intermingled;
there's still
in the staggering feet the gesture of tamed greeting.

Let the frenzy of your lovers swell ever so high--
let your taverns for once be real.
Soon will the supremacy of goods and chattel be over

as also the heavy burden of cares,

even if the chains keep on clanking forever.

Méré Hamdam! Méré Dost!

Gar mujhé i's ka yaqin ho méré
    hamdam, méré dost
gar mujhe is ka yaqin ho ke téré dil
    ki thakan
téri ankhoṅ ki udasi, téré sin'é ki
    jalan
méri diljo'i, méré pyar sé mit ja'égi
gar méra harf-é tasalli voh dava ho
    jis sé
ji uthe phir téra, ujra hu'a bé-noor
    damagh
téri peshani sé dhul jā'éin yé tazlil
    ké dagh
teri bimar javani ko shifa hoj'āé
gar mujhe i's ka yaqin ho mére
    hamdam, mere dost!
roz-o-shab, sha'm-o-sahar main
    tujhe baihlata rahoon
main tujhe gīt sunata rahoon halké,
    shirin
absharoṅ ké baharon ké, chaman-
    zaroṅ ké gīt
āmad'é subh' ké, mahtab ké,
    sayyaron ke gīt

tujh sé main husn-o-mohabbat ki
    hikayāt kahooṅ
kaisé maghroor hasina'on ké barfāb
    sé jism
garm hathoṅ ki hararat mein pighal
    ja'té hain
kaisé ék chéhré ké thaihré hu'é
    mānoos nuqoosh
dékhté dekhté yak-lakht badal ja'té
    hain
kis tar'h ariz-é mahboob ka shaffaf
    billaur
yék bayak bada-é-ahmar sé daihek
    jata hai
kaisé gulchin ké liyé jhukti hai
    khud shākh-é gulāb
kis tar'h rāt ka aivān mahek jata hai

مرے ہمدم! میرے دوست!

گر مجھے اس کا یقیں ہو مرے ہمدم، مرے دوست!
گر مجھے اس کا یقیں ہو کہ ترے دل کی تھکن
تیری آنکھوں کی اداسی، ترے سینے کی جلن
میری دلجوئی، مرے پیار سے مٹ جائے گی
گر مر احرف تسلی وہ دوا ہو جس سے
جی اٹھے پھر ترا، اجڑا ہوا بے نور دماغ
تیری پیشانی سے دھل جائیں یہ تذلیل کے داغ
تیری بیمار جوانی کو شفا ہو جائے
گر مجھے اس کا یقیں ہو مرے ہمدم، مرے دوست!
روز و شب، شام و سحر میں تجھے بہلا تار ہوں
میں تجھے گیت سنا تار ہوں ہلکے شیریں
آبشاروں کے بہاروں کے، چمن زاروں کے گیت
آمد صبح کے، مہتاب کے، سیاروں کے گیت

تجھ سے میں حسن و محبت کی حکایات کہوں
کیسے مغرور حسیناؤں کے برف سے جسم
گرم ہاتھوں کی حرارت میں پگھل جاتے ہیں
کیسے اک چہرے کے ٹھہرے ہوئے مانوس نقوش
دیکھتے دیکھتے یک لخت بدل جاتے ہیں
کس طرح عارض محبوب کا شفاف بلور
یک بیک بادہ احمر سے دہک جاتا ہے
کیسے گلچیں کے لئے جھکتی ہے خود شاخ گلاب
کس طرح رات کا ایوان مہک جاتا ہے

My Friend, My Mate

If only I could be certain, my friend,
if only I could be sure that your heart's fatigue,
your eyes' despondency, your heartburn
will be healed by my consoling and my love,
>   if my word of cheer were the cure
>   to enliven your dull and desolate mind,
>   wash off the stains of humiliation
>   and heal your sick youth.
If only I could be certain, my friend,
I'd console you day and night, evening and morning,
humming to you songs, tender and sweet--
songs of waterfalls, of springs, of gardens,
of dawn's arrow, of the moon and the planets.
I'd tell you tales of beauty and love--of
the snow-cold bodies of proud and beautiful women
who melt in the heat of a passionate embrace –
how the still, familiar lines of a face
will change suddenly, unnoticed ;
how the crystal of the beloved's cheeks
takes on the glow of red wine;
how the rose-stem offers itself to the
>   flower-gatherer,
and how the hallway of night
is filled with fragrance.

یوں ہی گا تار ہوں، گا تار ہوں تیری خاطر

گیت بنتا ر ہوں، بیٹھا ر ہوں تیری خاطر

پر مرے گیت ترے دکھ کا مداوا ہی نہیں

نغمہ جراح نہیں، مونس و غم خوار سہی

گیت نشتر تو نہیں، مرہم آزار سہی

تیرے آزار کا چارہ نہیں نشتر کے سوا

اور یہ سفاک مسیحا رے قبضے میں نہیں

اس جہاں کے کسی ذی روح کے قبضے میں نہیں

ہاں مگر تیرے سوا، تیرے سوا، تیرے سوا

yoonhi gata rahoon, gata
    rahoon téri khatir
gīt bunta rahoon, bai'tha
    rahoon téri khatir
par méré gīt teré dukh ka
    mada'va hi nahin
naghma'h jarrah nahin,
    moonis-o-ghamkhar sahi
gīt nishtar to nahin, marham-é
    ā'zar sahi
téré a'zar ka chara'h nahin
    nishtar ké siva
aur yé saffāk masiha méré
    qabzé mein nahin
is jahan ké kisi zi-rooh ké qabze
    méin nahin
Hān magar téré siva, téré siva,
    téré siva

So would I keep on singing, sitting beside you,
weaving songs,
all for your sake.

But my songs are no cure for your pain--
a song is no surgeon even though it may be a
consoler;
music is no surgeon's knife even if it soothes
as a balm.
Your ailment has no cure save the lancet,
and this cruel cure is beyond me--
beyond anything that breathes on earth.
Yes, it rests with you,
only you!

Subh'e azādi

August '47

Yé dāgh dāgh ujala, yé shab-
    gazidah sahar

voh intezar tha jis ka, yé voh
    sahar t'o nahin

yé voh sahar t'o nahin jis ki arzoo
    le kar

cha'lé thay yar ké milja'égi kahin
    na kahin

falak ké dasht mein taron ki ākhri
    manzil

kahin t'o hoga shab-é sust'mauj
    ka sahil

kahin to ja'ké rukéga safina'h-é-
    gham-é dil

javan lahoo ki pur-asrar
    shahrahon sé

cha'lé jo yār t'o dāman pé kitné
    hāth paré

dayar-é-husn ki bé-sabr
    khab-gahon sé

pukarti rahin bāhein, badan
    bulāté rahé

bahut azīz thi lekin rukh-é-sahar
    ki lagan

bahut qarin tha hasinan-é-noor ka
    dāman

subuk subuk thi tamanna, dabi
    dabi thi thakan

صبح آزادی

اگست 47ء

یہ داغ داغ اجالا، یہ شب گزیدہ سحر

وہ انتظار تھا جس کا، یہ وہ سحر تو نہیں

یہ وہ سحر تو نہیں جس کی آرزو لے کر

چلے تھے یار کہ مل جائے گی کہیں نہ کہیں

فلک کے دشت میں تاروں کی آخری منزل

کہیں تو ہو گا شبِ سست موج کا ساحل

کہیں تو جا کے رکے گا سفینۂ غمِ دل

جواں لہو کی پراسرار شاہراہوں سے

چلے جو یار تو دامن تو کتنے ہاتھ پڑے

دیارِ حسن کی بے صبر خواب گاہوں سے

پکارتی رہیں باہیں، بدن بلاتے رہے

بہت عزیز تھی لیکن رخِ سحر کی لگن

بہت قریں تھا حسینانِ نور کا دامن

سبک سبک تھی تمنا، دبی دبی تھی تھکن

The Morning of Freedom
August 1947

This daybreak, pockmarked--
this morning, night-bitten.
Surely, this is not the morning we'd longed for,
in whose eager quest, all comrades
had set out, hoping that somewhere
in the wilderness of the sky
would emerge the ultimate destination of stars;
somewhere, the wave of the slow night will meet
                         the shore
and somewhere will anchor the boat of
                         heart's grief.

As we friends set out on those mysterious highways
of young blood, how many hands caught us by
                         the sleeve?

From the dreamlands of beauty's pleasure-houses
kept beckoning to us, impatiently, seductive arms;
                         bodies called out to us.
But we yearned only for the morning's face,
ever. though within easy reach was the hem of
                         radiant beauties.
Delicate was our longing, and faint our sense of
                         exhaustion.

suna hai ho bhi chuka hai
  firaq-é-zulmat-o-noor
suna hai ho bhi chuka hai
  visa'l-é-manzil-o-gām
badal chuka hai bahut
  aihl-é-dard ka dastoor
nishat-é-vas'l halal-o azāb-é hijr
  harām

jigar ki āg, nazar ki umang, dil
  ki jalan
kisi pé charah-é-hijran ka kuch
  asar hi nahin
kahan sé ā'i nigār-e-saba,
  kidhar ko ga'ī
abhi charagh-é-sar-é-rah ko
  kuch khabar hi nahin

abhi girani-é shab méin kami
  nahin ā'ī
najat-é dida-o dil ki ghari nahin
  ā'ī
chalé chalo ké voh manzil abhi
  nahin ā'ī

سنا ہے ہو بھی چکا ہے فراق ظلمت و نور
سنا ہے ہو بھی چکا ہے وصال منزل و گام
بدل چکا ہے بہت اہل درد کا دستور
نشاط وصل حلال و عذاب ہجر حرام

جگر کی آگ، نظر کی امنگ، دل کی جلن
کسی پہ چارۂ ہجراں کا کچھ اثر ہی نہیں
کہاں سے آئی نگار صبا، کدھر کو گئی
ابھی چراغ سر رہ کو کچھ خبر ہی نہیں

ابھی گرانئ شب میں کمی نہیں آئی
نجاتِ دیدہ و دل کی گھڑی نہیں آئی
چلے چلو کہ وہ منزل ابھی نہیں آئی

We hear now that light and darkness have parted--
also, that there's now a union of quest and goal,
that the lot of the afflicted is now changed,
that the pleasure of union is granted
and banished is the torment of separation.

Fire in the bosom, longing in the eyes, and
                         heartburn--
nothing can soothe the anguish of separation.
Where did the sweet breeze come from, and where did
                        it vanish--
the street lamp has no news yet.
Even the night's heaviness is just the same;
the moment of salvation has not yet arrived
for the heart and the eye.

So let's press on, as the destination is still far away.

Lauh-o Qalam

لوح و قلم

Ham parvarish-é lauh-o qalam karte
    raheinge

jo dil pe guzarti hai raqam karte
    raheinge

asbab-é-gham-é-ishq bah'am karte
    raheingé

hān talkhi-e ayyam abhi aur baṛhe gi

hān aihl'ésitam, mashq-é sitam karte
    raheinge

manzoor yé talkhi, yé sitam ham ko
    gavarah

dam hai to madava-é sitam karte
    raheingé

mai-khana salamat hai to ham
    surkhi-e mai sé

taz'in-é dar-o bam-é haram karte
    raheingé

bakhi hai lahoo dil mein t'o har ashk
    se paida

rang-é lab-o rukhsar-é sanam karte
    raheinge

ek tarz-é taghaful hai so voh un ko
    mubarak

ek arz-é tamanna hai so ham karté
    rahéinge

ہم پرورش لوح و قلم کرتے رہیں گے

جو دل پہ گزرتی ہے رقم کرتے رہیں گے

اسبابِ غمِ عشق بہم کرتے رہیں گے

ہاں تلخیِ ایام ابھی اور بڑھے گی

ہاں اہلِ ستم، مشقِ ستم کرتے رہیں گے

منظور یہ تلخی، یہ ستم ہم کو گوارا

دم ہے تو مداوائے ستم کرتے رہیں گے

مے خانہ سلامت ہے تو ہم سرخیِ مے سے

تزئینِ درو بامِ حرم کرتے رہیں گے

باقی ہے لہو دل میں تو ہر اشک سے پیدا

رنگِ لبِ و خسارِ صنم کرتے رہیں گے

اک طرزِ تغافل ہے سو وہ ان کو مبارک

اک عرضِ تمنا ہے سو ہم کرتے رہیں گے

Pen and Paper

Forever will I nurture pen and paper,
forever express in words whatever my heart undergoes,
forever proffer ingredients of the sorrows of love
and quicken into life the wasteland of time.

Yes, the bitterness of time will keep on spawning,
just as the tyrants will persist in their cruelty.

Cheerfully, I'll give in to bitterness, this tyranny too
                         I'll endure -
so long as there's breath, I'll seek ever new cures
                    for torments.
If the tavern still remains, I shall embellish every door
and balcony of the *haram* with the redness of wine.

If the heart is not drained of all blood, I'll colour
                    every tear
with the redness of the beloved's lips and cheeks.

This posture of indifference, let it be her prerogative--
for me it will always be my desire's entreaty.

Tum ā'é ho, na shab-é-intezar
    guzri hai
talāsh mein hai sahar, bār, bār
    guzri hai

junooṅ mein jitni bhi guzri ba'kar
    guzri hai
agarche'h dil pé kharabi hazār
    guzri hai

hu'i hai hazrat-é-nāseh sé
    guftugoo jis shab
voh shab zaroor sar-é koo'é yar
    guzri hai

voh bāt saré fasané mein jis ka zikr
    na tha
voh bāt un ko bahut nagavar guzri
    hai

na gul khilé hain, na u'n sé milé,
    na māi pi hai
ajib rang méin ab ké bahār guzri
    hai

chaman pé gharat-e gulchin se
    ja'né kya guzri
qafas sé āj saba be-qarar guzri hai

تم آئے ہو، نہ شب انتظار گزری ہے
تلاش میں ہے سحر، بار، بار گزری ہے

جنوں میں جتنی بھی گزری بکار گزری ہے
اگر چہ دل پہ خرابی ہزار گزری ہے

ہوئی ہے حضرتِ ناصح سے گفتگو جس شب
وہ شب ضرور سرِ کوئے یار گزری ہے

وہ بات سارے فسانے میں جس کا ذکر نہ تھا
وہ بات ان کو بہت ناگوار گزری ہے

نہ گل کھلے ہیں، نہ ان سے ملے، نہ سے پی ہے
عجیب رنگ میں اب کے بہار گزری ہے

چمن پہ غارتِ گلچیں سے جانے کیا گزری
قفس سے آج صبا بے قرار گزری ہے

Neither Have You Come

Neither have you come, nor has ended the long
                         night of wait.
Even the breeze has whisked about, time and again,
                         seeking you.

Whatever time's spent in frenzy is well spent ,
even if the heart has taken on a thousand
                    mishaps.

The night spent in confabulation with the adviser
was surely the one spent also down the beloved's lane.
        What was never intended in the tale
        is primarily that which has piqued her most.
No flowers blooming, no rendezvous, no wine--
how strangely has spring passed away this time.

Nobody knows what befell the garden, in
                  the wake
of the flower-gatherer's pillage--
so restlessly has the breeze flit past the
                  nest today.

Tumhari yād ke jab zakhm bharne
    lagte hain
kisi bahane tumhein yad karne
    lagte hain
hadis-e yar ke unvan nikharne
    lagte hain
t'o har harim mein gesoo sanvarne
    lagte hain
har ajnabi hamein maihram dikhai
    deta hai
jo ab bhi teri gali se guzarne lagte
    hain
saba se karte hain ghurbat nasib
    zikr-e vatan
t'o chashm-e subh' mein ānsoo
    ubharne lagte hain
voh jab bhi karte hain i's nutq-o lab
    ki bakhyagari
faza mein aur bhi naghme bikharne
    lagte hain
dar-e-qafas pe andhere ki moh'r
    lagti hai
t'o Faiz dil me sitare utarne lagte
    hain

تمہاری یاد کے جب زخم بھرنے لگتے ہیں
کسی بہانے تمہیں یاد کرنے لگتے ہیں
حدیثِ یار کے عنواں نکھرنے لگتے ہیں
تو ہر حریم میں گیسو سنورنے لگتے ہیں
ہر اجنبی ہمیں محرم دکھائی دیتا ہے
جواب بھی تیری گلی سے گزرنے لگتے ہیں
صبا سے کرتے ہیں غربت نصیب ذکرِ وطن
تو چشمِ صبح میں آنسو ابھرنے لگتے ہیں
وہ جب بھی کرتے ہیں اس نطق و لب کی بخیہ گری
فضا میں اور بھی نغمے بکھرنے لگتے ہیں
درِ قفس پہ اندھیرے کی مہر لگتی ہے
تو فیض دل میں ستارے اترنے لگتے ہیں

When the Scars of Memory Begin to Heal

When the scars of memory begin to heal,
I think of you on one pretext or the other.
As the word of my beloved blossoms
every woman begins to groom her hair.
Every stranger appears to be a confidant,
even now when I pass through your lane.
Whenever the exiles talk to the breeze of their
                                  homeland,
tears well up in the morning's eyes.
Whenever our lips are sewn up
still more the air resounds with songs.
As darkness seals the prison door,
stars illumine the heart, O Faiz.

Shafaq ki rākh mein jal bujh gaya
  sitara-e sham

shab-e firaq ke gesoo faza mein
  lahra'e

koi pukaro ke ek umr ho'ne ā'ī
  hai!

falak ko qafila-e roz-o shām
  thaihra'e

ye zid hai yād-e harifan-e bādah
  paima ki

ke shab ko chānd na nikle na din
  ko ab'r ā'e

Saba ne phir dar-e-zindan pe ā'ke
  di dastak

sahar qarib hai, dil se kaho na
  ghabrā'e

شفق کی راکھ میں جل بجھ گیا ستارۂ شام
شبِ فراق کے گیسو فضا میں لہرائے
کوئی پکارو کہ اک عمر ہونے آئی ہے!
فلک کو قافلۂ روز و شام ٹھہرائے
یہ ضد ہے یاد حریفانِ بادہ پیما کی
کہ شب کو چاند نہ نکلے نہ دن کو ابر آئے
صبا نے پھر درِ زنداں پہ آ کے دی دستک
سحر قریب ہے، دل سے کہو نہ گھبرائے

The Evening Star Has Burnt Out

The evening star has burnt out in dusk's ashes--
in the air wave the locks of the parting night.

Let someone proclaim life is running itself out,
the sky has held up the caravan of morning and
                              evening.

This is their obduracy, these enemies of wine
                      and cup--
let there be no moon by night, no cloud by day.

The breeze has knocked at the prison door again:
dawn is about to break, tell the heart not to feel
                      so restive.

D'o Ishq

دو عشق

(1)

(۱)

Tāza'h hain abhi yād méin a'i saqi-é
gulfām
voh aks-e ru<u>kh</u>-é yar sé laihke hu'é
ayyam
voh phool si khilti hu'i dīdar ki sa'at
voh dil sa dharakta hu'a ummīd ka
hangam
ummīd ke lo jaga <u>gh</u>am-e dil ka
nasiba'h
lo shauq ki tarsi hu'i shab ho'gaī
ākhir
lo doob ga'é dard ke bé<u>kh</u>ab sitar'é
ab chamke'ga bé-sab'r nigahon ka
muqaddar
is bām se nikle ga tere husn ka
khurshīd
is kunj sé phoote'gi kiran, rang-o
hina ki
is dar sé baihe'ga téri raftar ka
sīmab
is rah pé phoole'gi shafaq teri qaba
ki
phir dékhe hain voh hij'r ké tapte
hu'é din bhi
jab fikr-é dil-o jan mein fughan
bhool ga'i hai
har shab voh siyah bojh ké dil bai<u>th</u>
gaya hai
har subh' ki lau tīr si sin'é mein lagi
hai
tanhai mein kya kya na tujhé yad
kya hai
kya kya na dil-é zār né dhoondi
hain panahéin

تازہ ہیں ابھی یاد میں اے ساقی گلفام
وہ عکس رخ یار سے لہکے ہوئے ایام
وہ پھول سی کھلتی ہوئی دیدار کی ساعت
وہ دل ساد ھڑ کتا ہوا امید کا ہنگام
امید کہ لو جاگا غم دل کا نصیبہ
لو شوق کی ترسی ہوئی شب ہو گئی آخر
لو ڈوب گئے درد کے بے خواب ستارے
اب چمکے گا بے صبر نگاہوں کا مقدر
اس بام سے نکلے گا ترے حسن کا خورشید
اس کنج سے پھوٹے گی کرن، رنگ حنا کی
اس در سے بہے گا تیری رفتار کا سیماب
اس راہ پہ پھولے گی شفق تیری قبا کی
پھر دیکھے ہیں وہ ہجر کے تپتے ہوئے دن بھی
جب فکر دل و جاں میں فغاں بھول گئی ہے
ہر شب وہ سیہ بوجھ کہ دل بیٹھ گیا ہے
ہر صبح کی لو تیر سی سینے میں لگی ہے
تنہائی میں کیا کیا نہ تجھے یاد کیا ہے
کیا کیانہ دل زار نے ڈھونڈی ہیں پناہیں

Two Loves

I

Still green are the memories, O beautiful cup-bearer–
those days glowing with reflections from that face,
the moment of meeting, like a bud opening out,
that instant of hope, like a heart-throb.

Lo, the heartache is now recompensed,
ending at last the night's yearning.
Lo, the dreamless stars of pain are gone,
now the eager eyes' fortune will be rekindled.

From the terrace will emerge your beauty's sun,
from that niche shoot out the ray of henna's tint;
from this doorstep will flow your footstep's quicksilver,
and on that pathway glow your tunic's twilight.

Again have I also seen those scorching days of parting
when lament had forgotten itself, brooding over love
                              and life.

Each night--so much burden wearing down my heart,
each morning's glow, piercing the heart like an arrow.

How often have I remembered you in my loneliness,
how many shelters has my aggrieved heart not sought?

ānkhon se lagaya hai kabhi dast-é-
saba ko
dāli hain kabhi gardan-é-mahtab
mein bahein
(2)
chaha hai isi rang mein laila-é-vatan
ko
tarpa hai isi taur sé dil i'ski lagan
mein
dhoondi hai yonhi shauq né
asa'ish-é-manzil
rukhsar ké kham mein kabhi kakul ki
shikan mein
is jan-é jahān ko bhi yonhi qalb-o
nazar né
hans hans ké sada di, kabhi ro ro ké
pukara
pooré kiyé sab harf-é tamanna ké
taqazé
har dard ko ujyala, har ek gham ko
sanvara
vapas nahin phera koi farman junoon
ka
tanha nahin lauti kabhi avaz jaras ki
khairiyat-é-jan, rahat-é-tan, sehat-é
daman
sab bhool ga'ien maslehatein aihl-é
havas ki
i's rah mein jo sab pé guzarti hai voh
guzri
tanha pas-é zindan, kabhi rusva sar-é
bazar
Garjé hain bahut shaikh sar-e gosha-é
mimbar
Karké hain bahut aihl-e- huk'm
barsar-é-darbar
chora nahin ghairon ne koi navak-é
dushnam
chooti nahin apnon sé koi
tarz-é-malamat
i's ishq, na u's ishq pé nadim hai
magar dil
har dāgh hai is dil mein ba'juz
dagh-é-nadamat

Sometimes I have let the breeze's palm caress my eyes
and sometimes put my arms around the moon's nape.

II
Just so, have I craved for my Laila, my land,
my heart fluttered with the same longing;
just so has passion sought fulfilment--
sometimes in the cheek's curve, at times in the
                    lock's curl.
And so have the heart and the eye called out to
                    the other beloved,
sometimes through laughter, at times through tears -
and fulfilled all demands of desire;
kindled every pain and cared for every sorrow.
Never turned down any of frenzy's commands,
never renounced all worldly compromises--
life's security, body's comfort, hem's safety.

Much has the priest roared from the pulpit,
and much has the ruler thundered in the open court.
Never did my enemies share the barb of abuse
nor did my friends forsake their style of censure.

I have no regrets over this love or that--
my heart carries all the stains--
except remorse.

Nisar main téri galyon ke.......

نثار میں تیری گلیوں کے ....

Nisar main téri galyon ké a'i vatan
ké jahan

chali hai rasm ke koi na sar uthaké
chalé

jo koi chahné vala tavaf k'o niklé

nazar chura ké chalé, jism-o jan
bacha ké cha'lé

hai aihl-é dil ké liyé ab ye naz'm-é
bast-o kushad

ké sang-o-khisht muqayyad hain aur
sag azad

bahut hai zulm ké dast-é bahana'joo
ké liyé

jo chand aihl-é-junoon tére nām'leva
hain

bané hain aihl-é havas, mud'da'i bhi,
munsif bhi

kise vakil karein, kis sé munsifi
chahein

magar guzārne valon ke din guzarte
hain

tere firaq mein yoon subh-o sham
karté hain

bujha jo rauzan-é-zindan t'o dil yé
samjha hai

ké téri mang sitaron se bhar'gai hogi

chamak uthey hain salasil t'o ham né
jana hai

ké ab sahar tére rukh par bikharga'i
hogi

نثار میں تری گلیوں کے اے وطن کہ جہاں
چلی ہے رسم کہ کوئی نہ سر اٹھا کے چلے
جو کوئی چاہنے والا طواف کو نکلے
نظر چرا کے چلے، جسم و جاں بچا کے چلے
ہے اہل دل کے لئے اب یہ نظم بست و کشاد
کہ سنگ و خشت مقید ہیں اور سگ آزاد
بہت ہے ظلم کے دست بہانہ جو کے لئے
جو چند اہل جنوں تیرے نام لیوا ہیں
بنے ہیں اہل ہوس، مدعی بھی، منصف بھی
کسے وکیل کریں، کس سے منصفی چاہیں
مگر گزرنے والوں کے دن گزرتے ہیں
ترے فراق میں یوں صبح و شام کرتے ہیں

بجھا جو روزن زنداں تو دل یہ سمجھا ہے
کہ تیری مانگ ستاروں سے بھر گئی ہوگی
چمک اٹھے ہیں سلاسل تو ہم نے جانا ہے
کہ اب سحر ترے رخ پر بکھر گئی ہوگی

Dedicated to Your Alleyways

I'm dedicated to your alleyways, O my motherland,
where it's customary now that nobody may walk
                                   about, head held high.
If anyone dare step out, he must do so in furtive fear
                                   of body and soul.
All your devotees must now withstand a new law,
                                   a new order--
"Stones and bricks enchained, but dogs out at large."

There's enough to provoke tyranny's hand, seeking
                                   pretexts--
those few ardent devotees who still cherish your name.
These power-mongers are now both judges and
                                   petitioners--
who then will defend us, and where shall we seek
                                   justice?

But there are some who must perforce spend their days
banished from you, this is how their mornings and
                                   evenings grind on.

As the cell's slit grows dim
my heart imagines your hair studded with stars,
and as the fetters become visible,

dawn, I imagine, must have lit up your face.

gharaz tasavvur-é sham-o sahar
  mein jīté hain
girift-é-saya-é divar-o-dar méin
  jite hain
yonhi hamésha ulajhti rahi hai
  zulm sé khalq
na u'n ki rasm na'i hai, na apni rīt
  na'ī
Yonhi hamésha khila'é hain ham
  né āg mein phool
na un ki hār na'ī hai na apni jīt na'ī
isi sabab se falak ka gila nahin
  karté
téré firaq mein ham dil bura nahin
  karte

gar aj tujh se juda hain t'o kal
  baham hongé
ye rāt bhar ki juda'i to koi bāt
  nahin
gar āj auj pé hai ta'le-é-raqib to kya
yeh char din ki khuda'i to koi bāt
  nahin
jo tujh sé aih'd-e vafa ustuvār
  rakhte hain
ilaj-é gardish-e lail-o-nahar rakhté
  hain

غرض تصورِ شام و سحر میں جیتے ہیں
گرفتِ سایۂ دیوار و در میں جیتے ہیں
یوں ہی ہمیشہ الجھتی رہی ہے ظلم سے خلق
نہ ان کی رسم نئی ہے، نہ اپنی ریت نئی
یوں ہی ہمیشہ کھلائے ہیں ہم نے آگ میں پھول
نہ ان کی ہار نئی ہے نہ اپنی جیت نئی
اسی سبب سے فلک کا گلہ نہیں کرتے
ترے فراق میں ہم دل برا نہیں کرتے

گر آج تجھ سے جدا ہیں تو کل بہم ہوں گے
یہ رات بھر کی جدائی تو کوئی بات نہیں
گر آج اوج پہ ہے طالعِ رقیب تو کیا
یہ چار دن کی خدائی تو کوئی بات نہیں
جو تجھ سے عہدِ وفا استوار رکھتے ہیں
علاجِ گردشِ لیل و نہار رکھتے ہیں

73

So I live on these fantasies, held by the shadows
of doors and walls, mornings and evenings.

The same age-old war between tyrants and mankind--
never have their ways changed, nor ours.
Always, we have let flowers bloom in fire.
It's always been the same--their defeat, our triumph.
That's why we've no grievance against our destiny,
no gloom over our separation from you.

If today we part, tomorrow's for reunion--
this brief spell of a night's separation is no matter.
If the rival's star towers high today,
this transient supremacy is of no consequence.
Only those committed to you deeply
hold the answer to the whirligig of time.

Dil mein ab yoon téré bhoolé hu'é
gham a'té hain

jaisé bichré hu'e ka'bé mein sanam
ā'té hain

ek ek karké hu'e ja'té hain tar'é
raushan

meri manzil ki taraf téré qadam ā'té
hain

raqs-é mai téz karo, saz ki lai téz
karo

soo'é maikhana safiran-é-haram ā'té
hain

kuch hamin ko nahin, ehsan uthane
ka.damagh

voh t'o jab ā'té hain, ma'il ba-karam
ā'té hain

aur kuch der na guzré
shab-é-furqat sé kaho

dil bhi kam dukhta hai, voh yad bhi
kam ā'té hain

دل میں اب یوں ترے بھولے ہوئے غم آتے ہیں

جیسے بچھڑے ہوئے کعبے میں صنم آتے ہیں

ایک اک کر کے ہوئے جاتے ہیں تارے روشن

میری منزل کی طرف تیرے قدم آتے ہیں

رقص مے تیز کرو، ساز کی لے تیز کرو

سوئے مے خانہ سفیرانِ حرم آتے ہیں

کچھ ہمیں کو نہیں، احسان اٹھانے کا دماغ

وہ تو جب آتے ہیں، مائل بہ کرم آتے ہیں

اور کچھ دیر نہ گزرے شبِ فرقت سے کہو

دل بھی کم دکھتا ہے، وہ یاد بھی کم آتے ہیں

In My Heart Now Well Up

In my heart now well up your long-forgotten sorrows
as though some forsaken idol returns to the *kaaba*.

One by one the stars are coming alive--
your footfalls are drawing close to my destination.

Pep up the tempo of the wine-dance, let the music
                            swell to its crescendo--
to the tavern come the emissawries of the *haram*.

It is I alone who would not seek favours,
although she is even willing to oblige.

Tell the night of separation to hold itself awhile,
for the heart now aches less and remembrance too
                          is faint.

Ab vohi harf-e-junoon sab ki zaban
    thaihri hai
jo bhi chal nikli hai voh bāt kahan
    thaihri hai

āj tak shaikh ke ikram mein jo sha'i
    thi haram
ab vohi dushman-e dīn rahat-e jan
    thaihri hai

hai khabar garm ke phirta hai
    guraizan nāseh
guftugoo aj sar-e koo-e butan
    thaihri hai

hai vohi ariz-e laila vohi shīrin ka
    daih'n
nigah-e shauq ghari bhar ko jahān
    thaihri hai

vas'l ki shab thi t'o kis darjah subuk
    guzri thi
hijr ki shab hai to kya sakht gīran
    thaihri hai
ek dafa bikhri to hath ā'ī hai kab
    mauj-e shamim
dil se nikli hai to kya lab pe fughan
    thaihri hai

اب وہی حرفِ جنوں سب کی زباں ٹھہری ہے
جو بھی چل نکلی ہے وہ بات کہاں ٹھہری ہے

آج تک شیخ کے اکرام میں جو تھی حرام
اب وہی دشمنِ دیں راحتِ جاں ٹھہری ہے

ہے خبر گرم کہ پھر تا ہے گریزاں ناصح
گفتگو آج سرِ کوئے بتاں ٹھہری ہے

ہے وہی عارض لیلیٰ وہی شیریں کا دہن
نگہہ شوق گھڑی بھر کو جہاں ٹھہری ہے

وصل کی شب تھی تو کس درجہ سبک گزری تھی
ہجر کی شب ہے تو کیا سخت گراں ٹھہری ہے
اک دفعہ بکھری تو ہاتھ آئی ہے کب موجِ شمیم
دل سے نکلی ہے تو کیا لب پہ فغاں ٹھہری ہے

It's the same word of Passion

It's the same word of passion on everybody's lips;
how can a word be muzzled once it gets moving
around?

Till today, whatever was held taboo in the priest's
esteem,
the same has now become the unbeliever's credo, the
soul's repose.

It's strongly rumoured that the adviser is dodging
everyone,
for today he's engaged to hold a talk down the
beloved's lane.

There's the same Laila's cheek, the same mouth of
Shirin,
on whomsoever has the fond eye settled for a moment.

The night of union--how fast it sped past;
and the night of separation, how very burdensome it is.

Once diffused, how can the wave of fragrance be
recaptured;
once out of the heart, when has lament stayed on
the lips?

dast-é sayyad bhi ajiz hai kaf-é
gulchin bhi
boo-é gul <u>th</u>aihri, na bulbul ki
zaban <u>th</u>aihri hai

ā'té ā'té yonhi dam bhar ko ruki
hogi bahar
ja'té ja'té yonhi pal bhar ko
khizan <u>th</u>aihri hai

ham ne jo tarz-é-fughan ki hai
qafas mein ījad
Faiz gulshan mein vohi
tarz-é-bayan <u>th</u>aihri hai

دستِ صیاد بھی عاجز ہے کفِ گلچیں بھی
بوئے گل ٹھہری، نہ بلبل کی زباں ٹھہری ہے

آتے آتے یوں ہی دم بھر کو رکی ہو گی بہار
جاتے جاتے یوں ہی پل بھر کو خزاں ٹھہری ہے

ہم نے جو طرزِ فغاں کی ہے قفس میں ایجاد
فیض گلشن میں وہی طرزِ بیاں ٹھہری ہے

Helpless is the bird-killer's hand, so also the flower-
gatherer's--
nothing has stayed on, not the scent of a rose, nor
the nightingale's song.

In its smooth coming, spring must have paused for
a moment,
and in its going, stalled autumn momentarily.

The style of lament I innovated in captivity--
that mode, O Faiz, has caught on everywhere in the
garden.

ā'é kuch abr, kuch sharab ā'é

is ke ba'd ā'é jo azāb ā'é

bām-é-mina sé māhtab ut'ré

dast-é saqi mein āftab ā'é

har rag-é-khoon mein phir
    charaghan ho

samné phir voh bé-naqab ā'é

um'r ke har varaq pe dil ko nazar

teri mehr-o-vafa ké bāb ā'é

kar-raha tha gham-é jahān ka
    hisāb

āj tum yād be-hisāb ā'é

na ga'ī teré gham ki sardari

dil méin yoon roz inquilab a'é

jal uthe bazm-é ghair ké
    dar-o-bām

jab bhi ham khānuman kharab ā'é

i's tar'h apni khamushi goonji

goya har simt se javāb ā'é

Faiz thi rāh sar'basar manzil

ham jahān pahunché kāmyab ā'é

آئے کچھ ابر، کچھ شراب آئے

اس کے بعد آئے جو عذاب آئے

بام مینا سے ماہتاب اترے

دست ساقی میں آفتاب آئے

ہر رگ خوں میں پھر چراغاں ہو

سامنے پھر وہ بے نقاب آئے

عمر کے ہر ورق پہ دل کو نظر

تیری مہر و وفا کے باب آئے

کر رہا تھا غم جہاں کا حساب

آج تم یاد بے حساب آئے

نہ گئی تیرے غم کی سرداری

دل میں یوں روز انقلاب آئے

جل اٹھے بزم غیر کے در و بام

جب بھی ہم خانماں خراب آئے

اس طرح اپنی خامشی گونجی

گویا ہر سمت سے جواب آئے

فیض تھی راہ سر بسر منزل

ہم جہاں پہنچے کامیاب آئے

Let There Be Some Clouds

Let there be some clouds, some wine
and then if retribution follows, who cares?

Let the moon descend to the terrace
and in the cup-bearer's palm appear the sun.

Let candles light up in every blood-vein
as she appears, her face unveiled.

On every page of the book of life, my heart saw
a sequence of the cantos of your kindness and loyalty.

Counting today the sorrows of this world –
endlessly I remembered you.

Never could I challenge your love's daily supremacy
even though revolt has been my heart's daily wont.

Up in flames went my rival's concourse – roof and
                            doors,
each time my destitute self showed up there.

Such was the resonance of my silence,
it seemed answers echoed from all directions.

Fully triumphant was my life's journey, O Faiz,
success greeted me wherever I went.

Zindan ki ek shām

زنداں کی ایک شام

Shām ke pech-o khām, sitaron se
Zina'h zina'h utar rahi hāi rat
yoon saba pas se guzarti hai
jaise kaih di kisi ne pyar ki bāt
saihn-e-zindan ke be-vatan ashjar
sarnigoon, maih'v hain banane mein
dāman-e āsman pe naqsh-o-nigar
shanah-e-bam par damakta hai
meh'rban chandni ka dast-e-jamīl
khak mein ghul ga'ī hai āb-e-nujoom
noor mein ghul gaya hai arsh ka nīl
sabz goshon mein nilgoon sā'e
lahlahate hain jis tar'h dil mein
mauj-e dard-e firaq-e yār ā'e
dil se paiham khayal kaihta hai
itni shirin hai zindagi is pal
zulm ka zaih'r ghol'ne va'le
kamran ho'sakein'ge aj na kal
jalva gah-e visal ki sham'ein
voh bujha bhi chuke agar t'o kya
chānd ko gul karein t'o ham jānein

Prison: One Evening

From the sinuous pathways of evening stars,
the night climbs down, step by step.
From close-by, the breeze streams past
as though someone has dropped a word of love.
In the prison courtyard, the trees--exiled,
heads drooping, absorbed in embroidering the
       sky's hem.
On the terrace's shoulder, blazes
benign moonlight's beautiful hand.
In the dust is dissolved the stars' lustre
and the sky's turquoise is suffused with light.
In the green niches sway blue reflections
as if the heart is swayed by the parting ache.

Ceaselessly wells up in my heart the thought--
how very sweet this instant is.
those busy concocting poison
   will succeed
neither today nor tomorrow.

What if you have put out the candles
in our luminous chamber of love--
snuff out the moon
and I'll concede defeat.

Yād

یاد

Dasht-e tanha'ī mein a'i jan-e-jahan,
    larzan hain

دشتِ تنہائی میں، اے جانِ جہاں، لرزاں ہیں

teri avaz ke sā'e, tere honton ke
    sarab

تیری آواز کے سائے، تیرے ہونٹوں کے سراب

dasht-e-tanhai mein doori ke
    <u>kh</u>as-o <u>kh</u>ak ta'le

دشت تنہائی میں دوری کے خس و خاک تلے

khil rahe hain, tere paihloo ke
    saman aur gulab

کھل رہے ہیں، ترے پہلو کے سمن اور گلاب

uth rahi hai kahin qurbat se teri
    sans ki ānch

اٹھ رہی ہے کہیں قربت سے تری سانس کی آنچ

apni <u>kh</u>ushboo mein sulagti hoi
    madham madham

اپنی خوشبو میں سلگتی ہوئی مدھم مدھم

door ufaq par, chamakti hoi qatrah
    qatrah

دور افق پار، چمکتی ہوئی قطرہ قطرہ

gir-rahi hai teri dildar nazar ki
    shabnam

گر رہی ہے تری دل دار نظر کی شبنم

is qadar pyar se, a'i jan-e-jahan
    rakha hai

اس قدر پیار سے، اے جانِ جہاں رکھا ہے

dil ke ru<u>kh</u>sar pe is vaqt teri yād ne
    hāth

دل کے رُخسار پہ اس وقت تری یاد نے ہات

yoon guman hota hai, garche'h hai
    abhi sub'h-e firaq

یوں گماں ہوتا ہے، گرچہ ہے ابھی صبح فراق

dhal gaya hij'r ka din, ā hi ga'i vas'l
    ki rāt

ڈھل گیا ہجر کا دن، آ ہی گئی وصل کی رات

85

Remembrance

In the wilderness of my heart, O love,
waver
the shadows of your voice
the mirages of your lips.
In the desert of loneliness --
there, under the remote dust and straw of separation--
are unfolding the jasmines and roses of your lap.

There rises, from closeby, the flame of your breath
glowing softly in its own heady fragrance.
And there, beyond the horizon, falls
drop by drop, the effulgent dew
of your alluring glance.

O my love, with such tenderness
has your memory's hand caressed the cheeks
of my heart that it appears, as if,

although it is still the dawn of separation,
the day of parting has faded away
and the night of love's union has just arrived.

sham-e-firaq ab na pooch, a'i aur a
    ke tal ga'i

dil tha ke phir baihal gaya, jan thi
    ke phir sambhal ga'i

bazm-e-khayal mein tere, husn ki
    sham'a jal ga'i

dard ka chand bujh gaya hijr ki rat
    dhal ga'i

jab tujhe yad karliya, sub'h maihek
    maihek uthi

jab tera gham jaga liya, rat machal
    machal ga'i

dil se t'o har moa'malah kar ke
    cha'le thay saf ham

kaihne mein u'n ke samne ba't
    badal badal ga'i

akhir-e shab ke hamsafar Faiz na
    jane kya hu'e

rah ga'i kis jagah saba, sub'h kidhar
    nikal ga'i

شامِ فراق اب نہ پوچھ، آئی اور آ کے ٹل گئی
دل تھا کہ پھر بہل گیا، جاں تھی کہ پھر سنبھل گئی

بزم خیال میں ترے، حسن کی شمع جل گئی
درد کا چاند بجھ گیا ہجر کی رات ڈھل گئی

جب تجھے یاد کر لیا، صبح مہک مہک اٹھی
جب ترا غم جگالیا، رات مچل مچل گئی

دل سے تو ہر معاملہ کرکے چلے تھے صاف ہم
کہنے میں ان کے سامنے بات بدل بدل گئی

آخرِ شب کے ہم سفر فیض نجانے کیا ہوئے
رہ گئی کس جگہ صبا، صبح کدھر نکل گئی

Ask Me Not About the Evening of Parting

Ask me not about the evening of parting--it came and
passed--
it was the heart that again felt cosoled
and it was life that regained its poise.

In my fancy was kindled your beauty's flame--
gone was the moon of pain, gone the night of
separation.

Whenever I remembered you, the morning came alive,
fragrant
and whenever I revived your sorrow, the night went
restive.

With my heart I'd already settled what to say--
but when it came to saying it there, the words veered
and hedged.

Faiz, my fellow travellers of the night's last hours,
what happened to them?
where did the breeze part company and where did the
morning vanish?

Mulaqāt

ملاقات

ye rāt u's dard ka shajar hai
jo mujh se tujh se azim'tar hai
azim'tar hai ke i's ki shakhon
mein lakh mash'al ba'kaf sitaron
ke karvan, ghir ke kho ga'e hain
hazar mahtab, i;s ke sa'e
mein apna sab noor ro ga'e hain
ye rāt u's dard ka shajar hai
jo mujh se tujh se azim'tar hai
magar isi rāt ke shajar se
ye chand lamhon ke zard pat'te
gir'e hain aur tere gesoo'on mein
ulajh ke gulnar ho ga'e hain
isi ki shabnam se khamushi ke
ye chand qatre, teri jabin par
baras ke, hīr'e piroga'e hain
bahut siyah hai ye rāt le'kin
isi siyahi mein roonuma hai
voh naihr-e-khoon jo meri sada hai
isi ke sā'e mein noorgar hai
voh mauj-e zar jo teri nazar hai

یہ رات اس درد کا شجر ہے
جو مجھ سے تجھ سے عظیم تر ہے
عظیم تر ہے کہ اس کی شاخوں
میں لاکھ مشعل بکف ستاروں
کے کارواں، گھر کے کھو گئے ہیں
ہزار مہتاب، اس کے سائے
میں اپنا سب نور، رو گئے ہیں
یہ رات اس درد کا شجر ہے
جو مجھ سے تجھ سے عظیم تر ہے
مگر اسی رات کے شجر سے
یہ چند لمحوں کے زرد پتے
گرے ہیں اور تیرے گیسووں میں
الجھ کے گلنار ہو گئے ہیں
اسی کی شبنم سے خامشی کے
یہ چند قطرے، تری جبیں پر
برس کے، ہیرے پرو گئے ہیں
بہت سیہ ہے یہ رات لیکن
اسی سیاہی میں رونما ہے
وہ نہر خوں جو مری صدا ہے
اسی کے سائے میں نور گر ہے
وہ موج زر جو تری نظر ہے

89

Rendezvous

This night is that pain's tree
which towers higher than you or me--
higher it is, for in its boughs are lost
the caravans of a hundred thousand torch-bearing
stars;
a thousand moons have, under its shadow, wailed
over the loss of their lustre.

This night is that pain's tree
which towers higher than you or me;
but from this very tree have fallen
the pallid leaves of these few moments;
tangled in your locks, they have blossomed into
scarlet.
From this very dew have fallen
a few drops of silence on your forehead
and are now strung into pearls.

Ebony dark is the night
but truly in this darkness emerges
that river of blood which is my cry,
and just under its shadow is that illuminator,
the rich wave of gold--
your eye.

Voh gham jo is vaqt téri bahon

ke gulsitan mein sulag raha hai

(voh gham jo is rāt ka samar hai)

kuch aur tap jā'é apni āhon

ki anch mein t'o yehi sharar hai

har ek siyah shakh ki kaman se

jigar mein toote hain tīr jitne

jigar se noche hain, aur har ek

ka ham ne tīsha'h bana liya hai

alam'nasibon, jigar' figaron

ki sub'h, aflak par nahin hai

jahan pe ham tum kharé hain donon

sahar ka raushan ufaq yahin hai

yahin pe gham ke sharar khil kar

shafaq ka gulzar ban ga'é hain

yahin pe qatil dukhon ke ti'she

qatār andar qatār kirnon

ke atishin har ban ga'e hain

ye gham jo is rāt ne diya hai

ye gham sahar ka yaqin bana hai

yaqin jo gham sé karim tar hai

sahar jo shab sé azīm tar hai

وہ غم جو اس وقت تیری باہوں

کے گلستاں میں سلگ رہا ہے

(وہ غم جو اس رات کا ثمر ہے)

کچھ اور تپ جائے اپنی آہوں

کی آنچ میں تو یہی شرر ہے

ہر ایک سیہ شاخ کی کماں سے

جگر میں ٹوٹے ہیں تیر جتنے

جگر سے نوچے ہیں، اور ہر اک

کا ہم نے تیشہ بنا لیا ہے

الم نصیبوں، جگر فگاروں

کی صبح، افلاک پر نہیں ہے

جہاں پہ ہم تم کھڑے ہیں دونوں

سحر کا روشن افق یہیں ہے

یہاں پہ غم کے شرار کھل کر

شفق کا گلزار بن گئے ہیں

یہیں پہ قاتل دکھوں کے تیشے

قطار اندر قطار کرنوں

کے آتشیں ہار بن گئے ہیں

یہ غم جو اس رات نے دیا ہے

یہ غم سحر کا یقیں بنا ہے

یقیں جو غم سے کریم تر ہے

سحر جو شب سے عظیم تر ہے

That sorrow which is smouldering, this moment,
in the rose-garden of your arms
(that sorrow which is the night's fruition),
if tempered a little more in the fire of our sighs,
would turn into a flame.

From the bow of every dark branch,
whatever arrows have pierced my heart,
I've plucked them out, forged each into a hatchet.

The dawn of the ill-fated and the heart-broken
is not up there in the sky,
but right here where you and I stand--
here glows the bright horizon of dawn.
It is here that sorrow's sparks have blossomed
into a garden of the crimson dusk,
and this is where the hatchets of fatal afflictions
have turned, rows within rows,
into the fiery garlands of sunbeams.

This very sorrow, boon of the night,
has lent us a faith for the future--
faith, far more bountiful than pain
and dawn, far grander than night.

Fikr-é sood-o ziyan t'o chooté gi

فکر سود و زیاں تو چھوٹے گی

minnat-é i'n-o-āṅ to choote gi

منت ایں و آں تو چھوٹے گی

khair, dozakh mein mai mi'lé na
    mi'lé

خیر، دوزخ میں سے ملے نہ ملے

shaikh saheb se jaṅ t'o choote gi

شیخ صاحب سے جاں تو چھوٹے گی

نہ آج لطف کر اتنا کہ کل گزر نہ سکے

وہ رات جو کہ ترے گیسوؤں کی رات نہیں

یہ آرزو بھی بڑی چیز ہے مگر ہمدم

وصال یار فقط آرزو کی بات نہیں

Na aj lutf kar itna ke kal guzar na
    saké

voh rāt jo ke teré gesoo'on ki rāt
    nahin

ye arzoo bhi bari chīz hai magar
    hamdam

visāl-é-yar faqat arzoo ki bāt nahin

Quatrains

At last I'll be rid of all concern for pain or loss –
also rid of the need to beseech all and sundry.
Never mind if there'll be no wine in hell -
at least the preacher will be nowhere around.

Grant me not so much bounty today that tomorrow
                    night, without your locks,
may become too wearisome.
Yearning is a great thing, O friend,
but union with the beloved is not just a matter of
                    longing.

Gulon méin rang bharé bad-é nau-
    bahar cha'le
cha'le bhi ā'o ke gulshan ka
    karobar cha'le

qafas udas hai yaro saba se kuch
    t'o kaho
kahin to baihr-e khuda āj
    zikr-é-yar cha'le

kabhi t'o sub'h téri kunj-é-lab se
    ho aghaz
kabhi t'o shab sar-é kakul se
    mushkbar cha'lé

bara hai dard ka rishta, yé dil
    gharib sahi
tumhare nam pe ā'énge
    ghamgusar cha'lé

jo ham pe guzri so guzri magar
    shab-é-hijran
hamaré ashk téri aqibat sanvar
    cha'lé

Huzoor-é-yar hu'i daftar-é junoon
    ki talab
girah mein léke gireban ka tar tar
    cha'lé

maqam Faiz koi rāh mein jacha hi
    nahin
jo koo-é-yār se nikle t'o soo-é dār
    cha'lé

گلوں میں رنگ بھرے بادِ نو بہار چلے
چلے بھی آؤ کہ گلشن کا کاروبار چلے

قفس اداس ہے یارو صبا سے کچھ تو کہو
کہیں تو بہرِ خدا آج ذکرِ یار چلے

کبھی تو صبح تری کنجِ لب سے ہو آغاز
کبھی تو شب سرِ کاکل سے مشکبار چلے

بڑا ہے درد کا رشتہ، یہ دل غریب سہی
تمہارے نام پہ آئیں گے غمگسار چلے

جو ہم پہ گزری سو گزری مگر شبِ ہجراں
ہمارے اشک تری عاقبت سنوار چلے

حضورِ یار ہوئی دفترِ جنوں کی طلب
گرہ میں لے کے گریباں کا تار تار چلے

مقام فیض کوئی راہ میں جچا ہی نہیں
جو کوئے یار سے نکلے تو سوئے دار چلے

Lending Colour to the Flowers

Lending hues to the flowers, blows the
spring breeze,
Now do come to let the garden blossom.

Sad is the cage, O friends, say something to the breeze,
somewhere, for God's sake, should be some talk
of the beloved today;

let the day break from the curl of your lips
and let the night go fragrant with the crest of your
lock.

Let the heart be humble--but deep is the bond of love;
if I invoke your name, many will come to commiserate
with me.

Whatever befell me, let it be; at least my tears,
O night of separation, had surely brightened you up.

Whenever my frenzy was summoned before my
love,
I appeared, my collar in shreds, as my lone asset.

No resting place, O Faiz, appealed all through the
journey;
as I emerged from my beloved's lane, I headed straight
for the gallows.

Sub'h phooti t'o asman pe tere
rang-e rukhsar ki phohar giri
rāt chā'i t'o roo-e alam par
teri zulfon ki abshar giri

Tamam shab dil-e-vaihshi talash
    karta hai
har ek sada mein tere harf-e-lutf
    ka ahang
har ek sub'h milati hai bar bar
    nazar
tere dahan se har ek lala o gulab
    ka rang

صبح پھوٹی تو آسماں پہ ترے
رنگ رخسار کی پھوہار گری
رات چھائی تو روئے عالم پر
تیری زلفوں کی آبشار گری

تمام شب دل وحشی تلاش کرتا ہے
ہر اک صدا میں ترے حرف لطف کا آہنگ
ہر ایک صبح ملاتی ہے بار بار نظر
ترے دہن سے ہر اک لالہ و گلاب کا رنگ

Quartrains

With the crack of dawn was sprayed in the sky
the roseate of your cheeks,
and with nightfall came down the cascade
of your tresses on the world's face.

All through the night, my wild heart craves
                              for you –
in every cry the harmony of your kind word.
Each morning my eye sees in your lips,
time and again, the tints of the tulip and the rose.

Daricha

دریچہ

Gaṛi hain kitni salibein mére dariché
    mein
Har ek apné masiha ke khooṅ ka
    rang liyé
Har ek vas'l-é-khudavand ki umang
    liyé

Kisi pe karté hain abr-é-bahar ko
    qurbaṅ
kisi pe qat'l mah-é.tabnak karte hain
Kisi pe hoti hai sarmast
    shakhsar-e-do nīm
Kisi pe bād-é-saba ko halak karte
    hain
Har ā'é din ye khudavandgan-é
    mehr-o-jamāl
Lahoo mein gharq mere ghamkadé
    mein ā'té hain
aur ā'é din méri nazron ke samne
    u'n ké
shahīd jism salamat utha'é jā'té hain

گڑی ہیں کتنی صلیبیں مرے دریچے میں
ہر ایک اپنے مسیحا کے خوں کا رنگ لئے
ہر ایک وصلِ خداوند کی اُمنگ کے لئے

کسی پہ کرتے ہیں ابر بہار کو قرباں
کسی پہ قتل مہ تابناک کرتے ہیں
کسی پہ ہوتی ہے سر مست شاخسار دو نیم
کسی پہ باد صبا کو ہلاک کرتے ہیں
ہر آئے دن یہ خداوندگان مہر و جمال
لہو میں غرق مرے غمکدے میں آتے ہیں
اور آئے دن مری نظروں کے سامنے ان کے
شہید جسم سلامت اٹھائے جاتے ہیں

Casement

How many crosses are fixed in my casement,
each tinged with the blood of its own messiah,
each yearning for union with God :

on one is sacrificed the spring's cloud,
the other held for the murder of the bright moon.
If for one the fruit-laden bough is beheaded,
for the other is killed the morning breeze.

Each new day, these gods of grace and beauty
visit my sorrowland, soaked in blood,
and each day, right before my eyes,
are carried away their martyred bodies.

Dard ā'e ga dabe Pā'on

درد آئے گا دبے پاؤں

Aur kuch der mein, jab phir mere
tanha dil ko
fikr ā'legi ke tanhai ka kya chara'h
kare
dard ā'e ga da'be pa'on liye surkh
charagh
voh jo ek dard dharakta hai kahin
dil se pa're

shola-e-dard jo paihloo mein lapak
uthe'ga
dil ki diwar pe har naqsh damak
uthe'ga
Halqa-e zulf kahin, gosha-e rukhsar
kahin
hij'r ka dasht kahin, gulshan-e-
didar kahin
lutf ki bat kahin, pyar ka iqrar
kahin

Dil se phir hogi meri bāt ke a'i dil
a'i dil
ye jo mahboob bana hai teri tanhai
ka
ye t'o mehman hai ghari bhar ka
chala ja'e ga
i's se kab teri musibat ka madava
ho'ga

Mushta'il ho ke bhi uthein'ge
vaihshi sā'e
ye chala ja'e ga rah jayenge baqi sā'e
rāt bhar jin se tera khoon kharaba
hoga
jang thaihri hai koi khel nahin hai
a'i dil
dushman-e-jan hain sabhi sare ke
sare qatil

Pain will creep in soft-footed

After a while, when my lonesome heart will once
                                again
be seized by angst, how shall I cure the loneliness?
Pain will then creep in soft-footed, carrying a red
                                taper---
that pain which throbs beyond the heart's precincts.

As this flame will leap forth in the side,
on the heart's wall will be rekindled every mark--
somewhere a lock's whorl, somewhere a cheek's curve,
somewhere the wilderness of parting, the joy
of seeing the beloved, a kind word, or love's assent.

Then will I say, O my heart,
this thought, the beloved of your loneliness,
is only a visitant for a moment--
so how can your problem be solved?

After it's gone, will rise enraged
savage shadows, which will linger on
for me to battle with all through the night.

This is a war, O my heart, not a frolic;
all your life's enemies, all your assassins--

Ye kaṛi rāt bhi, ye sa'é bhi, tanhai bhi
dard aur jang mein kuch mel nahin
    hai a'i dil
la'o sulgao koi josh-é ghazab ka angar

taish ki atish-é jarrar kahan hai la'o
voh daihekta hu'a gulzar kahan hai
    la'o
jis méin garmi bhi hai harkat bhi
    tavana'i bhi

ho na ho apné qabilé ka bhi koi
    lashkar
muntazir hoga andheré ki fasilon ké
    udhar

In ko sholo'n ké rajaz apna pata to
    deinge
khair, ham tak voh na pahunchein bhi
    sada to deingé
dōōr kitni hai abhi sub'h, bata to
    deingé

یہ کڑی رات بھی، یہ سائے بھی، تنہائی بھی
درد اور جنگ میں کچھ میل نہیں ہے اے دل
لاؤ سلگاؤ کوئی جوش غضب کا انگار

طیش کی آتش جرار کہاں ہے لاؤ
وہ دہکتا ہوا گلزار کہاں ہے لاؤ
جس میں گرمی بھی ہے حرکت بھی توانائی بھی

ہو نہ ہو اپنے قبیلے کا بھی کوئی لشکر
منتظر ہوگا اندھیرے کی فصیلوں کے اِدھر

ان کو شعلوں کے رجز اپنا پتا تو دیں گے
خیر، ہم تک وہ نہ پہنچیں بھی صدا تو دیں گے
دور کتنی ہے ابھی صبح، بتا تو دیں گے

this harsh night, these shadows, this loneliness.
There's nothing common between pain and war,
                    O my heart.
Fetch me an ember of fierce passion and kindle it,
get me from somewhere the mighty flame of wrath
with its heat, its dynamism, its puissance.

Maybe a limb of our tribe is waiting
on the other side of the ramparts of darkness.
Let's alert our comrades of our presence
through fiery martial songs.
Well, even if they don't reach us, they'll call out to us
to intimate how far the dawn still is.

Rāt dhalne lagi hai sīnon mein

āg sulgao ābginon mein

dil-e ushaq ki khabar lena

phool khilte hain in mahinon mein

رات ڈھلنے لگی ہے سینوں میں

آگ سلگاؤ آبگینوں میں

دل عشاق کی خبر لینا

پھول کھلتے ہیں ان مہینوں میں

āj tanha'i kisi hamdam-é-derin ki

   tar'h

karne ā'i hai meri saqi gari shām

   dhalé

muntazir baithe hain ham donon ke

   mahtāb ubhré

aur tera aks jhalakne lagé har sa'é

    ta'lé

آج تنہائی کسی ہمدم دیریں کی طرح

کرنے آئی ہے مری ساقی گری شام ڈھلے

منتظر بیٹھے ہیں ہم دونوں کہ مہتاب ابھرے

اور ترا عکس جھلکنے لگے ہر سائے تلے

Quatrains

The night's fading away in the bosoms--
stoke up the fire in the goblets.
Take care of lovers' hearts--
these are the months for flowers to bloom.

Today loneliness, like an old friend, has come
to do some cupbearing for me, at dusk.
We're both lying in wait for the moon to rise--
and your reflections to flash in every shadow.

Koi āshiq kisi māhbooba sé

کوئی عاشق کسی محبوبہ سے!

Yād ki rah'guzar jis pé isi soorat
se
muddatein bīt ga'i hain tumhein
chalte chalte
khatm ho'ja'é jo do char qadam
aur chalo
mo'r parta hai jahan dasht-é-
faramoshi ka
jis se a'ge na koi main hoon na
koi tum ho
sāns tha'mé hain nigahein ke na
jane kis dam
tum palat ā'o, guzar ja'o ya mur
kar dekho

garche'h vaqif hain nigahin ké yé
sab dhoka hai
gar kahin tum sé ham-aghosh hoi
phir sé nazar
phoot niklégi vahan aur koi
rāhguzar
phir isi tar'h jahan hoga muqabil
paiham
saya-é zulf ka aur jumbish-é
bazoo ké safar

doosri bāt bhi jhooti hai ke dil
janta hai
yan koi mor koi dasht koi ghat
nahin
jis ké parde mein mera māh-é-
ravān doob saké
tum sé chalti rahé yé rah, yonhi
acha hai
tum né mur kar bhi na dékha to
koi bāt nahin

یاد کی راہ گزر جس پہ اسی صورت سے
مدتیں بیت گئی ہیں تمہیں چلتے چلتے
ختم ہو جائے جو دو چار قدم اور چلو
موڑ پڑتا ہے جہاں دشتِ فراموشی کا
جس سے آگے نہ کوئی میں ہوں نہ کوئی تم ہو
سانس تھامے ہیں نگاہیں کہ نہ جانے کس دم
تم پلٹ آؤ، گزر جاؤ، یا مڑ کر دیکھو

گرچہ واقف ہیں نگاہیں کہ یہ سب دھوکا ہے
گر کہیں تم سے ہم آغوش ہوئی پھر سے نظر
پھوٹ نکلے گی وہاں اور کوئی راہ گزر
پھر اسی طرح جہاں ہو گا مقابل پیہم
سایہ زلف کا اور جنبشِ بازو کا سفر

دوسری بات بھی جھوٹی ہے کہ دل جانتا ہے
یاں کوئی موڑ کوئی دشت کوئی گھات نہیں
جس کے پردے میں مرا ماہِ رواں ڈوب سکے
تم سے چلتی رہے یہ راہ، یوں ہی اچھا ہے
تم نے مڑ کر بھی نہ دیکھا تو کوئی بات نہیں

107

Some lover to his beloved

This path of memory on which you have been trudging
for ages
if you press on a few steps further, it will wind off
to where one encounters the wilderness of oblivion,
at the bend beyond which neither I exist, nor you.
The eyes hold their breath and wonder
if you'd return, pass by, or look back.

Although the eyes know it's all an illusion
still, if they encounter you again somewhere,
a new pathway will branch out
where will begin again, as in the past,
the journey of your lock's shadow
and my outstretched arm.

The other thing is also a delusion, that the heart
knows
there's no curve, no wilderness, no ambush
behind whose screen could sink my sailing moon.
Well, it's good that this journey with you runs on;
it wouldn't matter even if you didn't look back.

Teri umid tera intezar jab se hai

na shab ko din se shikayat na din
   ko shab se hai

kisi ka dard ho karte hain tere nam
   raqam

gila hai jo bhi kisi se tere sabab se
   hai

hu'a hai jab se dil-e-na'saboor
   be-qaboo

kalam tujh se nazar ko bare adab se
   hai

Agar sharar hai to bharke, jo phool
   hai to khile -

tar'h tar'h ki talab, tere rang-e-lab se
   hai

kahan ga'e shab-e-furqat ke jagne
   vale

Sitara-e-sahari ham-kalam kab se
   hai

تری امید ترا انتظار جب سے ہے

نہ شب کو دن سے شکایت نہ دن کو شب سے ہے

کسی کا درد ہو کرتے ہیں تیرے نام رقم

گلہ ہے جو بھی کسی سے ترے سبب سے ہے

ہوا ہے جب سے دل ناصبور بے قابو

کلام تجھ سے نظر کو بڑے ادب سے ہے

اگر شرر ہے تو بھڑکے ، جو پھول ہے تو کھلے

طرح طرح کی طلب، تیرے رنگ لب سے ہے

کہاں گئے شب فرقت کے جاگنے والے

ستارۂ سحری ہم کلام کب سے ہے

Ever Since I Have Been Waiting for You

Ever since I have been waiting for you,
buoyed up on hope,
neither has the night any grievance against the day
nor the day against the night.
Anybody else's pain, I attribute to you,
and you are the cause of my grudge against anyone.
Ever since my rastless heart has gone out of control,
my eyes have learnt to converse with you,
                              deferentially.
If it's spark, let it leap out,
if a bud, let it blossom--
diverse are my demands from your crimson lips.
Where have they gone, those who kept awake during the
                              night of separation--
since when has the morning-star been engaged in a
                              colloquy?

Na dīd hai na sukhan, ab na harf hai
na payām

koi bhi hulya-é taskin nahin aur ās
bahut hai

umid-é-yar, nazar ka mizaj, dard ka
rang

tum āj kuch bhi na poocho ke dil
udas bahut hai

نہ دید ہے نہ سخن، اب نہ حرف ہے نہ پیام

کوئی بھی حلیہ تسکیں نہیں اور آس بہت ہے

امیدِ یار، نظر کا مزاج، درد کا رنگ

تم آج کچھ بھی نہ پوچھو کہ دل اداس بہت ہے

Quatrain

Not a glimpse of you--no word, no message
no ground for solace, yet hope unbounded.
Yearning for the beloved, the eye's mood, pain's
                                    hue--don't you
ask me anything today, the heart's brimful
                              with despair.

Shām

شام

Is tar'h hai ke har ek per koi
    mandir hai
koi ujra hu'a, be-noor purana
    mandir
dhoondta hai jo kharabi ke bahāne
    kab se
chāk har bām, har ek dar ka
    dam-é-akhir hai
āsman koi purohit hai jo har bām
    tale
jism par rākh ma'le, ma'the pe
    sindoor ma'le
sarnigoon bai'tha hai chup chap na
    ja'ne kab se
is tar'h hai ke pas-e parda koi sahir
    hai

jis ne āfaq pe phailaya hai yoon
    sāh'r ka dam
daman-e-vaqt se paivast hai yoon
    daman-é-sham
ab kabhi sham bujhe gi na andhéra
    hoga
ab kabhi rāt dhale gi na savera
    hoga

asman ās liye hai ke ye jadoo toote
chup ki zanjir kate, vaqt ka daman
    choote
de koi sankh dohai, koi payal bo'le
koi būt ja'ge, koi sāvnli ghoonghat
    kho'le

اس طرح ہے کہ ہر اک پیڑ کوئی مندر ہے
کوئی اجڑا ہوا، بے نور پرانا مندر
ڈھونڈتا ہے جو خرابی کے بہانے کب سے
چاک ہر بام، ہر اک در کا دم آخر ہے
آسماں کوئی پروہت ہے جو ہر بام تلے
جسم پر راکھ ملے، ماتھے پہ سیندور ملے
سرنگوں بیٹھا ہے چپ چاپ نہ جانے کب سے
اس طرح ہے کہ پس پردہ کوئی ساحر ہے

جس نے آفاق پہ پھیلایا ہے یوں سحر کا دام
دامن وقت سے پیوست ہے یوں دامن شام
اب کبھی شام بجھے گی نہ اندھیرا ہو گا
اب کبھی رات ڈھلے گی نہ سویرا ہو گا

آسماں اس لیے ہے کہ یہ جادو ٹوٹے
چپ کی زنجیر کٹے، وقت کا دامن چھوٹے
دے کوئی سنکھ دہائی، کوئی پائل بولے
کوئی بت جاگے، کوئی سانولی گھونگھٹ کھولے

Evening

It's as though each tree is a temple--
ruined, unlit, old--
seeking, for long, justification for its decadence.
Every terrace ripped apart, every door at its last breath.
The sky a priest, sits under each terrace,
body smeared with ash, forehead hued with vermilion,
head drooping, mute--nobody knows since when.
It's as though there's some conjuror behind the screen
who has flung across the sky a net of magic.
So closely linked is time's hem with that of
                             the evening
that it may never fade away, nor darkness
                                 ever descend –
now this night will never pass, nor dawn ever break.

The sky is propped up on the hope that
the spell may soon be over,
the chain of silence snap,
time's hem come unstuck--
that some conch may blare out for help, some

                                     ankle-bells speak out,
some idol come alive, some dusky beauty unveil her face.

Ham khasta tanon se mohtasibo
kya mal-o-manal ka poochte ho
jo umr se ham ne bhar paya sab
sāmne lā'e dete hain
daman mein hai musht-e khak-e
jigar saghar mein hai khoon-e
hasrat-e mai
lo ham ne daman jhāṛ diya, lo jām
ulta'e dete hain

ہم خستہ تنوں سے محتسبو کیا مال و منال کا پوچھتے ہو

جو عمر سے ہم نے بھر پایا سب سامنے لائے دیتے ہیں

دامن میں ہے مشت خاک جگر ساغر میں ہے خون

حسرت مے

لو ہم نے دامن جھاڑ دیا، لو جام الٹائے دیتے ہیں

Quartain

We are the enfeebled, what's there to ask about our
                    assets, O Censors.
All that life has proffered us, we're holding up
                    for scrutiny:
In the hem a handful of the heart's dust, in the
        goblet the blood of yearning's wine.
Look, here we empty our hem, and here we upturn
                    the wine-glass.

Kab thaihre ga dard a'i dil kab rāt
  basar hogi
sunte thay voh ā'enge sunte thay
  sahar hogi

kab jān lahoo hogi, kab ashk gohar
  hoga
kis din teri shunvai a'e dīda-é tar
  hogi
kab maihke'gi fas'l-é gul kab
  baihke'ga maikhana
kab sub'h-é sukhan hogi kab
  sham-é-nazar hogi
va'iz hai na zahid hai, na'séh hai na
  qa'til hai
ab shaihr mein yaron ki kis tar'h
  basar hogi
kab tak abhi rah dekhein a'i qamat-é
  jānāna'h
kab hashr mo'ayyan hai tujh ko t'o
  khabar hogi

کب ٹھہرے گا درد اے دل کب رات بسر ہو گی
سنتے تھے وہ آئیں گے سنتے تھے سحر ہو گی

کب جان لہو ہو گی، کب اشک گہر ہو گا
کس دن تری شنوائی اے دیدۂ تر ہو گی
کب مہکے گی فصلِ گل کب بہکے گا میخانہ
کب صبح سخن ہو گی کب شامِ نظر ہو گی
واعظ ہے نہ زاہد ہے، ناصح ہے نہ قاتل ہے
اب شہر میں یاروں کی کس طرح بسر ہو گی
کب تک ابھی رہ دیکھیں اے قامت جانانہ
کب حشر معین ہے تجھ کو تو خبر ہو گی

117

When Will Pain Cease?

When will pain cease, O heart, when will the night
                            pass away?
It was rumoured that she'd come; and it would soon
                            be dawn.

When will life turn into blood, and tears become
                            pearls?
And when will you be heard, O my tearful eye?

When will the flowers bloom, and when will the
                            tavern go heady?
When will morning inspire verse, and when will
                            evening bring us together?

No preacher, no ascetic, no counsellor, no assassin--
how will it now fare with the lovers in town?

How long will I keep looking for you, O my beloved?
When is that doomsday ordained, surely you'd know.

be'dam hū'é bīmar dava kyoon
    nahin déte

Tum aché masiha ho, shifa kyoon
    nahin déte

dard-é-shab-é-hijran ki jaza kyoon
    nahin déte

khoon-é dil-é vaihshi ka sila
    kyoon nahin déte

mit jae'gi makhlooq t'o insaf
    karo'gé

munsif ho t'o ab hashr utha kyoon
    nahin déte

hān nuktah'varo lā'o lab-o dil ki
    gavahi

hān naghma'garo saz-é sada
    kyoon nahin déte

Paiman-é-junoon hathon ko
    sharma'éga kab tak

dil valo, giréban ka pata kyoon
    nahin déte

barbadi-é-dil jab'r nahin Faiz kisi
    ka

voh dushman-é-jan hai to bhula
    kyoon nahin déte

بے دم ہوئے بیمار دوا کیوں نہیں دیتے
تم اچھے مسیحا ہو، شفا کیوں نہیں دیتے

درد شب ہجراں کی جزا کیوں نہیں دیتے
خون دل وحشی کا صلہ کیوں نہیں دیتے

مٹ جائے گی مخلوق تو انصاف کرو گے
منصف ہو تو اب حشر اٹھا کیوں نہیں دیتے
ہاں نکتہ وَرو لاؤ لب و دل کی گواہی
ہاں نغمہ گرو ساز صدا کیوں نہیں دیتے

پیمان جنون ہاتھوں کو شرمائے گا کب تک
دل والو، گریباں کا پتا کیوں نہیں دیتے
بربادی دل جبر نہیں فیض کسی کا
وہ دشمن جاں ہے تو بھلا کیوں نہیں دیتے

This Patient Breathless

This patient breathless, why don't you reclaim him?
A strange messiah are you, why don't you cure him?
Why is there no recompense for the aching night
                                of separation?
Why is there no reward for the sacrifice of love's
                                frenzy?
Will you dispense justice after mankind is
                                wiped out?
If you are a true judge, why not proclaim
                                doomsday today?
Call in the scar of pain, you discerners,
to bring up the testimony of speech and feeling,
and you music-makers, why don't you strike up
                                the song?
How long will frenzy's vow hold back its hand?
O lovers, why don't you point to the collar torn?
O Faiz, nobody compels you to endure the
                                heart's ravage;
if she's your heart's enemy, why don't you forget her?

Khatm hu'i bārish-é sang

ختم ہوئی بارشِ سنگ

Nagahan āj méré tar-é nazar sé katkar

tukṛé tukṛé hu'é āfāq pe khurshid-o qamar

ab kisi simt andhéra na ujala hoga

bujh ga'ī dil ki tar'h rāh-é vafa méré bād

dosto! qafila-é dard ka ab kya hoga

ab koi aur karé parvarish-é gulshan-é gham

dosto khat'm hu'ī dida-é tar ki shabnam

tham gaya shor-é junoon khat'm ho'i barish-é sang

khāk-é rah āj liyé hai lab-é dildar ka rang

Koo-é-jānān mein khula méré lahoo ka parcham

Dékhiyé deté hain kis kis ko sada méré bād

"Kaun hota hai harif-é mai-é mard afghan-é ishq

hai mukarrar lab-é saqi pé sala méré bad"

ناگہاں آج مرے تارِ نظر سے کٹ کر
ٹکڑے ٹکڑے ہوئے آفاق پہ خورشید و قمر
اب کسی سمت اندھیرانہ اجالا ہوگا
بجھ گئی دل کی طرح راہِ وفا میرے بعد
دوستو! قافلہ درد کا اب کیا ہوگا

اب کوئی اور کرے پرورش گلشن غم
دوستو ختم ہوئی دیدۂ تر کی شبنم
تھم گیا شور جنوں ختم ہوئی بارش سنگ
خاکِ رہ آج لئے ہے لبِ دلدار کا رنگ
کوئے جاناں میں کھلا میرے لہو کا پرچم
دیکھیے دیتے ہیں کس کس کو صدا میرے بعد
"کون ہو تا ہے حریفِ مے مردافگن عشق
ہے مکررلبِ ساقی پہ صلا میرے بعد"

121

End of the Rain of Stones

Suddenly, today, sundered from my vision's thread,
lay splintered in the sky the sun and the moon.
Now there'll be no light or darkness anywhere.
Extinguished, after me, like the heart, is the path of
                                commitment--
friends, how will it now fare with the caravan of pain?

Let somebody else now nurture the garden of sorrow;
friends, now has dried up the dew of the grieving eye,
now stalled frenzy's uproar, the rain of stones.
Today the pathway's dust carries the tint of the
                                beloved's lips,
and there stands unfurled, in her lane, the banner of
                                my blood.
Let's see which ones will be called out after I'm gone--
"Let's see who stands up to the fatal intoxication
                                of love,
for I still hear, from the cupbearer, the call for another
                                round, after I'm gone."

Kahān jāo'gé?

كہاں جاؤ گے ؟

Aur kuch dér mein lut ja'éga har
bām pé chānd
aks kho ja'éngé, ā'iné taras ja'engé
arsh ké dida-é namnak se bāri bāri
sab sitare sar-é khashak baras
ja'engé
ās ke māré thaké hāré shabistanon
méin
apni tanhā'i sameté ga bicha'éga koi
be-vafai ki ghaṛi, tark-é mudarat ka
vaqt
us ghaṛi apne siva, yād na ā'é ga koi
tark-é-dunya ka samān, khatm-é-
mulaqat ka vaqt
us ghaṛi a'i dil-é avārah kahān
jao'gé
us ghaṛi koi kisi ka bhi nahin rahné
d'o
koi us vaqt miléga hi nahin rahné
d'o
aur miléga bhi to i's taur ké pachtao
gé
u's ghaṛi a'i dil-é avarah kahan
jao'gé
aur kuch dér thaih'rjao ke phir
nashtar-é sub'h
zakhm ki tar'h har ék ankh ko bedar
karé
aur har kushta-é vamandagi-é
akhir-é-shab
bhool kar sa'at-é darmandagi-é
akhir-é shab
jan paihchan mulaqat pé israr kare

اور کچھ دیر میں لٹ جائے گا ہر بام پہ چاند

عکس کھو جائیں گے ، آئینے ترس جائیں گے

عرش کے دیدۂ نمناک سے باری باری

سب ستارے سر خاشاک برس جائیں گے

آس کے مارے تھکے ہارے شبستانوں میں

اپنی تنہائی سمیٹے گا بچھائے گا کوئی

بے وفائی کی گھڑی ، ترک مدارات کا وقت

اس گھڑی اپنے سوا،یاد نہ آئے گا کوئی

ترک دنیا کا ساں ، ختم ملاقات کا وقت

اس گھڑی اے دل آوارہ کہاں جاؤ گے

اس گھڑی کوئی کسی کا بھی نہیں رہنے دو

کوئی اس وقت ملے گا ہی نہیں رہنے دو

اور ملے گا بھی تو اس طور کہ پچھتاؤ گے

اس گھڑی اے دل آوارہ کہاں جاؤ گے

اور کچھ دیر ٹھہر جاؤ کہ پھر نشتر صبح

زخم کی طرح ہر اک آنکھ کو بیدار کرے

اور ہر کشتہ داماندگی کی آخرِ شب

بھول کر ساعت درماندگی کی آخرِ شب

جان پہچان ملاقات پہ اصرار کرے

Where Will You Go?

In just a short while, the moon will be robbed
on every terrace; reflections will fade away,
mirrors look insatiated; and from the sky's moist eye
will drop down on the dust all the stars, one by one.
In the jaded chambers of hope,
someone will fold up his loneliness, another spread
                              it out.
This is the moment of betrayal,
of brashness--this moment when
you'll be able to remember nobody else but yourself.
This is the mood for renouncing the world--
the moment of rendezvous' end.
Where will you go this moment, O my vagrant heart?
This moment, nobody is anybody's friend--so let it be;
nor will you meet anyone now--so let it be;
and even if you do, you will only regret it.

Hold back a little longer then, till dawn's lancet
opens up, like a wound, each eye
and every victim of the fatigue of the night's end
will insist on a friendly meeting,
forgetting the night's distress.

Jab teŕi samandar ānkhoṅ méin

جب تیری سمندر آنکھوں میں

Yé dhoop kinara, sham dha'lé
milté hain donoṅ vaqt jahāṅ
jo rāt na din, jo āj na kal
pal bhar ko amar, pal bhar mein
   dhu'āṅ
i's dhoop kinaŕé, pal d'o pal
hontoṅ ki lapak
bahoṅ ki chanak
yé mél hamara jhoot na sach
kyon raz karo, kyon dosh dharo
kis karan jhooti bāt karo
jab teri samandar ankhon méin
i's shām ka sooraj doobe'ga
sukh so'éin ge ghar dar vāḷé
aur rāhi apni rah léga.

یہ دھوپ کنارا، شام ڈھلے

ملتے ہیں دونوں وقت جہاں

جو رات نہ دن، جو آج نہ کل

پل بھر کو امر، پل بھر میں دھواں

اس دھوپ کنارے، پل دو پل

ہونٹوں کی لپک

باہوں کی چھنک

یہ میل ہمارا جھوٹ نہ سچ

کیوں راز کرو، کیوں دوش دھرو

کس کارن جھوٹی بات کرو

جب تیری سمندر آنکھوں میں

اس شام کا سورج ڈوبے گا

سکھ سوئیں گے گھر در والے

اور راہی اپنی رہ لے گا

In Your Ocean Eyes

The fringe of day, dusk
where the two hours of time meet--
neither night nor day, neither today nor tomorrow.
One moment eternal, another just smoke--
on this day's fringe, for a moment or two
the fervour of lips,
the ardour of arms,
this union of ours, neither true nor false.
Why say a false thing
when in your ocean eyes
will sink this evening's sun?
Then everyone will sleep blissfully in his house
and the traveller will wend his way.

Rang hai dil ka méré

رنگ ہے دل کا مرے

Tum na āé thay t'o har chīz vohi thi
ke jo hai

āsman had'd-é nazar, rāhguzar,
rāhguzar, shishah-é mai shisha-é
mai

aur ab shisha-é mai, rāhguzar,
rang-é-falak

rang hai dil ka méré, khoon-é jigar
ho'ne tak

champā'i rang kabhi rahat-é-didar
ka rang

surma'i rang ke hai sa'at-é bézar ka
rang

zard pattoon ka, khas-o khar ka rang

surkh phoolon ka daihekte ho
gulzar ka rang

zah'r ka rang, lahoo rang, shab-é tar
ka rang

āsman, rāhguzar, shisha-é mai,

koi bhiga hu'a daman, koi dukhti
hu'i rag

koi har lahza badalta hu'a ā'inah hai

ab jo āé ho t'o thaihro ké koi rang
koi rūt, koi sha'i

ek jagah par thaihré,

phir sé ek bar har ek chīz vohi ho ké
jo hai

āsman had'd-é nazar, rāhguzar
rāhguzar, shishah-é mai
shishah-é mai

تم نہ آئے تھے تو ہر چیز وہی تھی کہ جو ہے

آساں حدِ نظر، راہگزر راہگزر، شیشۂ مے شیشۂ مے

اور اب شیشۂ مے، راہگزر، رنگ فلک

رنگ ہے دل کا مرے، خون جگر ہونے تک

چمپئی رنگ کبھی راحتِ دیدار کا رنگ

سرمئی رنگ کہ ہے ساعت بیزار کا رنگ

زرد پتوں کا، خس و خار کا رنگ

سرخ پھولوں کا دہکتے ہوئے گلزار کا رنگ

زہر کا رنگ، لہو رنگ، شبِ تار کا رنگ

آساں، راہگزر، شیشۂ مے،

کوئی بھیگا ہوا دامن، کوئی دُکھتی ہوئی رگ

کوئی ہر لحظہ بدلتا ہوا آئینہ ہے

اب جو آئے ہو تو ٹھہرو کہ کوئی رنگ کوئی رُت، کوئی
شے

ایک جگہ پر ٹھہرے،

پھر سے اک بار ہر اک چیز وہی ہو کہ جو ہے

آساں حدِ نظر، راہگزر راہگزر، شیشۂ مے شیشۂ مے

The Colour of the Moment

Before you came, everything was what it is--
the sky, vision-bound
the pathway, the wine-glass.
And now the wine-glass, the pathway, the sky's tint--
everything bears the colour of my heart
till all melts into blood.
Sometimes the golden tinge, sometimes the hue of the
joy of seeing you
sometimes ashen, the shade of the dreary moment--
the colour of yellow leaves, of thorn and trash,
of the crimson petals of the flower-beds aglow,
the tint of poison, of blood, of sable night.
The sky, the pathway, the wine-glass--
some tear-stained robe, some wincing nerve,
some ever-revolving mirror.

Now that you're here, stay on
so that some colour, some season, some object
may come to rest
and once again everything may become what it was--
the sky, vision-bound, the pathway, the wine-glass.

Pās raho

پاس رہو

Tum mére pās raho
mére qatil mére dildar, mére pās
    raho
jis ghari rāt cha'le
āsmanon ka lahoo pī ke siyah rāt
    cha'le
marham-é mushk liye nashtar-é-
    almas liye
bain karti hu'i, hansti hu'i gati nikle
dard ke kāsni pazéb bajati nikle
jis ghari sīnon mein doobe hu'e dil
astinon méin nihan, hathon ki rah
    takne lagein
ās liyé,
aur bach'chon ke bilakné ki tar'h
    qulqul-é-mai,
baih'r-é-nāsoodagi machle to manā'é
    na mané,
jab koi bāt bana'é na bané
jab koi bāt cha'lé
jis ghari rāt cha'lé,
Jis ghari matami, sunsān, siyah rāt
    cha'lé
pās raho
mére qatil mere dildar mére pās
    raho

تم مرے پاس رہو

میرے قاتل مرے دلدار ، مرے پاس رہو

جس گھڑی رات چلے

آسمانوں کا لہو پی کے سیہ رات چلے

مرہم مشک لئے نشتر الماس لئے

بین کرتی ہوئی ، ہنستی ہوئی گاتی نکلے

درد کے کاسنی پازیب بجاتی نکلے

جس گھڑی سینوں میں ڈوبے ہوئے دل

آستینوں میں نہاں ، ہاتھوں کی رہ تکنے لگیں

آس لئے ،

اور بچوں کے بلکنے کی طرح قلقل مے ،

بہر ناسودگی مچلے تو منائے نہ منے ،

جب کوئی بات بنائے نہ بنے

جب کوئی بات چلے

جس گھڑی رات چلے ،

جس گھڑی ماتمی ، سنسان ، سیہ رات چلے

پاس رہو

میرے قاتل مرے دلدار مرے پاس رہو

Stay With Me

Stay with me--
my assassin, my sweetheart--stay on.
When the night moves on
after drinking the sky's blood,
when this dark night moves on
holding musk-balm,
diamond lancet.
Wailing, laughing, singing, it moves on--
jingling the purple anklets of pain.
When hearts sunk in bosoms
wait hopefully for hands
cloaked in sleeves,
and the wine gurgles like children's whining
when their desire once aroused,
no consoling will appease

when every word spoken fails to get across,
and no word gets moving forward,
when the night spins on,
when the mournful, dreary, dark night creeps on--
stay with me,
my assassin, my sweetheart, stay on.

Dīda-é-tar pé vahaṅ kaun nazar
  karta hai
kasa-é chashm mein khooṅ nab-é
  jigar lé ké chalo
ab agar jā'o pai-é arz-o talab u'n ké
  huzoor
dast-o kashkol nahin kasa-é sar lé
  ké chalo

دیدۂ تر پہ وہاں کون نظر کرتا ہے
کاسۂ چشم میں خوں ناب جگر لے کے چلو
اب اگر جاؤ پئے عرض و طلب ان کے حضور
دست و کشکول نہیں کاسہ سر لے کے چلو

Dīvar-é-shab aur aks-é rukh-é yar
  sāmné
phir dil ke ā'īné sé lahoo phootné
  laga
phir vaz'é ehtiyat sé dhundla ga'ī
  nazar
phir zabt-é arzoo sé badan tootné
  laga

دیوارِ شب اور عکس رخ یار سامنے
پھر دل کے آئینے سے لہو پھوٹنے لگا
پھر وضع احتیاط سے دھندلا گئی نظر
پھر ضبطِ آرزو سے بدن ٹوٹنے لگا

Quatrains

Who takes notice of the moist eye, there?
So go there, carrying in the eye's cup the heart's
        red blood.
Now if you go there with some entreaty, some craving,
carry not a beggar's but your skull's bowl.

The night's wall, and there in front the beloved's face
       reflected;
blood has again started oozing·from the heart's mirror;
again has caution blurred the gaze;
the body aches again from the muzzling of desire.

Yahān se' shaihr ko dékho!

يہاں سے شہر کو دیکھو!

Yahan se' shaihr ko dekho t'o halqah
    dar halqah

khinchi hai jail ki soorat har ek simt
    fasīl

har ek rāh'guzar gardish-é asirāṅ hai

na sang-é mīl, na manzil, na mukhlisi
    ki sabīl

jo koi téz cha'lé rāh t'o poochta hai
    khayal

ke tokne koi lalkar kyoon nahin ā'ī

jo koi hath hila'é t'o vahm ko hai
    saval

koi chanak, koi jhankar kyon nahin ā'ī

yahan se' shaihr ko dekho t'o sari
    khilqat mein

na koi saheb-é tamkin, na koi vāli-é
    hosh

har ek mard-é javan mujrim-é rasan
    ba' guloo

har ek hasina-é rana kaniz-é halqa
    bagosh

jo sā'é door charaghon ke' gird larzan
    hain

na' jane mahfil-é gham hai ke' bazm-é
    jām-o suboo

jo rang har dar-o divar par pareshan
    hain

yahan se' kuch nahin khulta ye phool
    hain ke' lahoo

یہاں سے شہر کو دیکھو تو حلقہ در حلقہ

کھنچی ہے جیل کی صورت ہر ایک سمت فصیل

ہر ایک راہ گزر گردشِ اسیراں ہے

نہ سنگ میل، نہ منزل، نہ مخلصی کی سبیل

جو کوئی تیز چلے رہ تو پوچھتا ہے خیال

کہ ٹوکنے کوئی للکار کیوں نہیں آئی

جو کوئی ہاتھ ہلائے تو وہم کو ہے سوال

کوئی چھنک، کوئی جھنکار کیوں نہیں آئی

یہاں سے شہر کو دیکھو تو ساری خلقت میں

نہ کوئی صاحبِ تمکیں، نہ کوئی والئی ہوش

ہر ایک مردِ جواں مجرم رسن بہ گلو

ہر اک حسینہ رعنا کنیز حلقہ بگوش

جو سائے دور چراغوں کے گرد لرزاں ہیں

نہ جانے محفل غم ہے کہ بزم جام و سبو

جو رنگ ہر در و دیوار پر پریشاں ہیں

یہاں سے کچھ نہیں کھلتا یہ پھول ہیں کہ لہو

Look at the City from Here

If you look at the city from here, you see
circles within circles;
every rampart like that of a prison
and every pathway a prisoner's circular walk--
no milestone, no destination, no way out.

If anyone walks fast, fancy asks:
why hasn't someone shouted to stop him?
And if somebody waves his hand, a doubt nags:
why hasn't anyone heard a chain clank?

If you look at the city from here, you'd realize
that in the entire crowd, there's nobody really
                          dignified,
nobody truly sagacious; every young man's neck
                    in a noose,
every woman a branded slave.

The shadows which waver round the distant lamps--
who knows if it's an assembly of grieving or
                          carousing men,
and all those hues which appear scattered on every
                    door and wall--
seen from here it could be the blood or flowers.

Blackout

بلیک آوٹ

Jab sé bé-noor hu'i hain sham'ein
khak mein dhoondta phirta hoon na
    jané kis ja
kho ga'i hain méri donon ankhein
tum jo vaqif ho batao koi paihchan
    méri
i's tar'h hai ke har ek rag mén utar
    aya hai
mauj dar mauj kisi zaih'r ka qatil
    darya
téra arman téri yad liye jan méri
jané kis mauj mein ghaltan hai kahan
    dil méra
ek pal thaihro ke is par kisi dunya sé
barq ā'é méri janib, yad-é-baiza lé kar
aur méri ankhon ké gumgashtah
    gohar
jam-é zulmat sé siyah mast
na'i ankhon ké shab-tāb gohar
    lauta dé
ek pal thaihro ke darya ka kahin pāt
    lagé
aur naya dil mera
zaih'r mein dhul ké fana ho ke kisi
    ghat lagé
phir pai-é nazr na'é dida-o-dil lé ké
    chaloon
Husn ki mad'h karoon, shauq ka
    mazmoon likhoon

جب سے بے نور ہوئی ہیں شمعیں

خاک میں ڈھونڈتا پھر تا ہوں نہ جانے کس جا

کھو گئی ہیں میری دونوں آنکھیں

تم جو واقف ہو بتاؤ کوئی پہچان مری

اس طرح ہے کہ ہر اک رگ میں اتر آیا ہے

موج در موج کسی زہر کا قاتل دریا

تیرا ارمان تری یاد لئے جان مری

جانے کس موج میں غلطان ہے کہاں دل میرا

ایک پل ٹھہرو کہ اس پار کسی دنیا سے :

برق آئے مری جانب، ید بیضالے کر

اور مری آنکھوں کے گم گشتہ گہر

جام ظلمت سے سیہ مست

نئی آنکھوں کے شب تاب گہر

لوٹا دے

ایک پل ٹھہرو کہ دریا کا کہیں پاٹ لگے

اور نیا دل میرا

زہر میں دھل کے فنا ہو کے

کسی گھاٹ لگے

پھر پے نذر نئے دیدہ و دل لے کے چلوں

حسن کی مدح کروں، شوق کا مضمون لکھوں

135

Blackout

Since the lamps have been snuffed out
I have been seeking in the dust:
somewhere I've lost both my eyes.
Since you know me, tell me some mark of my being.
It's as if into every vein has seeped
some lethal river of poison, wave after wave.
With my yearning for you, and remembrance,
O my love,
I wonder in which wave my heart has been wallowing.

Hold on for a moment, for
from across some world will flash toward me
lightning, with a luminous hand,
bringing back to me the lost pearls of my eyes
drunk on the cup of darkness--
my new night-illumining eyes.

Just hold on for a while so that
somewhere the river spreads itself out
and my nascent heart, abluted in poison, will perish
to resurrect itself and touch some wharf.
Then again will I set out, with the offering of a
new heart,
a new vision, to raise a hymn to beauty
and versify passion.

Soch'né d'o

سوچنے دو

Ik zara soch'né d'o
i's khayaban mein
jo i's lahza bayaban bhi nahin
kaun si shakh méin phool ā'é thay sab
    se paihlé
kaun be rang hu'i ranj-o ta'ab sé
    paihlé
aur ab sé paihlé

kis ghaṛi kaun sé mausam mein
    yahan
khoon ka qaih't paṛa
gul ki shah'rag pé kaṛa
vaqt paṛa
soch'ne d'o
ek zara soch'ne do
yé bhara shaihr jo ab vadi-é viran bhi
    nahin
i's mein kis vaqt kahan
āg lagi thi paihlé
i's ké saf basta darichon mein sé kis
    mein avval
zeh hu'i surkh shu'aon ki kaman
kis jagah jot jagi thi paihlé
soch'né d'o
ham sé i's des ka tum nam-o nishan
    poochté ho

اک ذرا سوچنے دو
اس خیاباں میں
جو اس لحظہ بیاباں بھی نہیں
کون سی شاخ میں پھول آئے تھے سب سے پہلے
کون بے رنگ ہوئی رنج و تعب سے پہلے
اور اب سے پہلے

کس گھڑی کون سے موسم میں یہاں
خون کا قحط پڑا
گل کی شہ رگ پہ کڑا
وقت پڑا
سوچنے دو
اک ذرا سوچنے دو
یہ بھرا شہر جو اب وادئ ویراں بھی نہیں
اس میں کس وقت کہاں
آگ لگی تھی پہلے
اس کے صف بستہ دریچوں میں سے کس میں اول
زہ ہوئی سرخ شعاؤں کی کماں
کس جگہ جوت جگی تھی پہلے
سوچنے دو
ہم سے اس دیس کا تم نام و نشاں پوچھتے ہو

Let Me Think

Let me think, just awhile--
in this garden
which at this moment is not even a wilderness,
on which bough sprouted the primal flowers
and which flower first blanched
with grief and fatigue?
And before this--
at which moment, and during which season
were we struck with the drought of blood
and the flower's jugular vein smarted
under time's harshness--
let me think.

Let me think a little.
This teeming city, now not even a
                              desolate valley--
here, when and where
did the first fire break out;
in which one of its arrayed windows
was first born the arc of blood-drenched flames –
and where did the first light flash?
let me think.

You ask me the whereabouts of that country

jis ki tarīkh na jughrafia ab yad ā'é

aur yad ā'é t'o mahboob-é guzishta ki
    tar'h

roobaro ā'né sé ji ghabra'é

han magar jaisé koi

aise mahboob ya mahbooba ka dil
    rakhne ko

ā nikalta hai kabhi rāt bitane ké liye

ham ab is umr ko ā pahunche hain jab
    ham bhi yonhi

dil sé mil a'té hain bas rasm nibhane
    ké liye

dil ki kya poochté ho

soch'ne d'o

جس کی تاریخ نہ جغرافیہ اب یاد آئے

اور یاد آئے تو محبوب گزشتہ کی طرح

روبرو آنے سے جی گھبرائے

ہاں مگر جیسے کوئی

ایسے محبوب یا محبوبہ کا دل رکھنے کو

آنکلتا ہے کبھی رات بتانے کے لئے

ہم اب اس عمر کو آپہنچے ہیں جب ہم بھی یوں ہی

دل سے مل آتے ہیں بس رسم نبھانے کے لئے

دل کی کیا پوچھتے ہو

سوچنے دو

whose history and geography now elude my memory
and, if at all recalled somehow,
it's like a beloved of the past
encountering whom, face to face,
the heart feels unnerved--

but yes, as if someone
just to cheer up his lover,
shows up sometime to spend the night.

I have now reached that point
when even if I go over to meet my beloved
it will be just for ritual's sake.

What's there to ask of my heart?--
let me think!

Heart Attack

ہارٹ اٹیک

Dard itna tha ke ūs rāt dil-é-vaihshi
    né

har rag-é-jan se ulajhna chaha

har bun-é moo sé tapakna chaha

aur kahin dōōr tére saih'n-é chaman
    mein goya

patta patta méré afsurdah lahoo
    mein dhul kar

husn-é mahtab se azurdah nazar
    a'né laga

méré virana-é tan méin goya

saré dukhte hu'e reshon ki tanabein
    khul kar

silsila'var patah déne lagīn

rukhsat-e qafila-é shauq ki tayyari
    ka

aur jab yād ki bujhti hu'i sham'on
    mein nazar ayā kahin

ek pal akhri lamha téri dildari ka

dard itna tha ke u's se bhi gūzarna
    chāha

ham né chāha bhi magar dil na
    thaiharna chāha

درد اتنا تھا کہ اس رات دل و حشی نے

ہر رگ جاں سے الجھنا چاہا

ہر بن مو سے ٹپکنا چاہا

اور کہیں دور ترے صحن چمن میں گویا

پتا پتا مرے افسردہ لہو میں دھل کر

حسن مہتاب سے آزردہ نظر آنے لگا

میرے ویرانہ تن میں گویا

سارے دکھتے ہوئے ریشوں کی طنابیں کھل کر

سلسلہ وار پتہ دینے لگیں

رخصت قافلہ شوق کی تیاری کا

اور جب یاد کی بجھتی ہوئی شمعوں میں نظر آیا کہیں

ایک پل آخری لمحہ تری دلداری کا

درد اتنا تھا کہ اس سے بھی گذرنا چاہا

ہم نے چاہا بھی مگر دل نہ ٹھہرنا چاہا

Heart Attack

Pain so intense that night, my savage heart
wanted to grapple with every artery,
and drip from every pore,

and out there, as though in your courtyard,
each leaf, bathed in my despondent blood,
began to look pale in the moonlight.

In my body's desert places, it seemed
as if, all the fibres of my wincing veins, undone,
began shooting out signals, ceaselessly--
preparations for the departure of love's caravan.

And when, in memory's fading lights,
there emergrd somewhere before the eye,
one last moment of your love's kindness--
the pain was so lacerating that
it ventured to overstep the moment.
I too willed to hold on to it,
but the heart would not agree.

Zabt ka aih'd bhi hai, shauq ka
    paiman bhi hai
aih'd-o-paiman se guzar jane ko ji
    chahta hai
dard itna hai ke har rag mein hai
    maih'shar barpa
aur sukoon aisa ke mar'jāne ko ji
    chahta hai

ضبط کا عہد بھی ہے، شوق کا پیمان بھی ہے

عہد و پیماں سے گزر جانے کو جی چاہتا ہے

درد اتنا ہے کہ ہر رگ میں ہے محشر برپا

اور سکوں ایسا کہ مر جانے کو جی چاہتا ہے

Quatrain

My vow of restraint, also my desire's covenant.
But I wish to move beyond both pledges and promises.
Pain so intense, there's a riot in every vein--
and such tranquillity that I'd rather cease to be.

Balin pe kahin rat dhal rahi hai
ya sham'a pighal rahi hai
paihloo mein koi chiz jal rahi hai
tum ho ke meri jan nikal rahi hai

ek sukhan mutrib-e zeba ke sulag
    uthe badan
ek qadah saqi-e madhosh jo kare
    hosh tamam
zikr-e subhe ke rukh-e yar se
    rangin tha chaman
yad-e shab'ha ke tan-e yar tha
    aghosh tamam

بالیں پہ کہیں رات ڈھل رہی ہے
یا شمع پگھل رہی ہے
پہلو میں کوئی چیز جل رہی ہے
تم ہو کہ مری جاں نکل رہی ہے

اک سخن مطرب زیبا کہ سلگ اٹھے بدن
اک قدح ساقی مہوش جو کرے ہوش تمام
ذکر صبح کہ رخ یار سے رنگیں تھا چمن
یاد شبہا کہ تن یار تھا آغوش تمام

Somewhere Near the Pillow

Somewhere near the pillow, the night's fading away
or is it the candle melting ?
Something is burning within me-
is that your memory, or my life
                              seeking to depart.

A verse from an enchanting singer that sets the
                              body afire--
a bowl of wine from an alluring cupbearer that may
                              turn your head;
a mention of the morning when the beloved's face lent
                              its colour to the garden;
the memory of the night when your beloved was
                              in your arms.

تہ بہ تہ دل کی کدورت

Taih b'a taih dil ki kudoorat
meri ānkhon mein umand ā' ī t'o
 kuch chārah na tha
chara'gar ki mān lī
aur main né gard'alood ānkhon ko
 lahoo sé dho liya
aur ab har shakl-o soorat

میری آنکھوں میں امنڈ آئی تو کچھ چارہ نہ تھا

چارہ گر کی مان لی

اور میں نے گرد آلود آنکھوں کو لہو سے دھولیا

میں نے گرد آلود آنکھوں کو لہو سے دھولیا

اور اب ہر شکل وصورت

ālam-é-maujood ki har ek sh'ai
Meri ānkhon ké lahoo sé i's tar'h
 hamrang hai
khurshīd ka kundan lahoo
mahtāb ki chāndni lahoo
sub'hon ka hansna bhi lahoo
rāton ka rona bhi lahoo
har shajar mīnar-é khoon,
har phool khoonin' dīdah hai
har nazar ek tār-é-khoon, har
 aks-é-é-khoon mālida hai
mauj-é khoon jab tak ravan rahti
 hai u'ska surkh rang
jazbah-é-shauq-é shahadat, dard
 ghaiz-o-gham ka rang
aur tham jā'yé t'o kujla kar
faqat nafrat ka, shab ka, maut ka
har rang ke mātam ka rang
chārah'gar aisa na honé dé
kahin se lā koi sailāb-é-ashk
jis mein vu'zoo
kar lein t'o shayad dhul sa'ké
meri ānkhon, meri gard ālood
 ānkhon ka lahoo

عالم موجود کی ہر ایک شئے

میری آنکھوں کے لہو سے اس طرح ہم رنگ ہے

خورشید کا کندن لہو

مہتاب کی چاندنی لہو

صبحوں کا ہنسنا بھی لہو

راتوں کا رونا بھی لہو

ہر شجر مینار خوں، ہر پھول خونیں دیدہ ہے

ہر نظر اک تار خوں، ہر عکس خوں مالیدہ ہے

موج خوں جب تک رواں رہتی ہے اس کا سرخ رنگ

جذبہ شوق شہادت، درد غیظ و غم کا رنگ

اور تھم جائے تو کجلا کر

فقط نفرت کا، شب کا، موت کا

ہر رنگ کے ماتم کا رنگ

چارہ گر ایسا نہ ہونے دے

کہیں سے لا کوئی سیلاب اشک

جس میں وضو

کریں تو شاید دھل سکے

میری آنکھوں، میری گرد آلود آنکھوں کا لہو

When the Heart's Bad Blood

When the heart's bad blood welled up, layer by layer,
in my eyes, there was no other way but to give in
to the counsellor,
and I washed my dust-filled eyes with blood.
And now every object of this sentient world
is so tinted with the blood of my eyes that
bloody is the sun's gold,
bloody the moon's silver
the morning's laughter,
the night's cries--
every tree is a minaret of blood
every flower blood-eyed,
every glance a streak of blood
every reflection blood-soaked.
So long as the blood flows in the vein, its red
is the red of the desire for martyrdom –
pain, rage or sorrow-
and if the flow ceases, it blackens
into mere hate, night, death--
into the mourning shade of every colour.
O my adviser, don't let this happen--
bring me from somewhere a deluge of tears
which may perhaps wash the blood
out of my eyes, my dust-filled eyes.

آرزو

Ārzoo

مجھے معجزوں پہ یقیں نہیں مگر آرزو ہے کہ جب قضا

مجھے بزم دہر سے لے چلے

تو پھر ایک بار یہ اذن دے

کہ لحد سے لوٹ کے آسکوں

ترے در پہ آکے صدا کروں

تجھے غمگسار کی ہو طلب تو ترے حضور میں آرہوں

یہ نہ ہو تو سوئے رہ عدم میں پھر ایک بار روانہ ہوں

Mujhé mo'jizoń pe yaqiń nahiń
    magar arzoo hai ke jab qaza
mujhe bazm-é daihr se lé cha'lé
t'o phir ek bar ye izn de
ke laihd se laut ké ā'sakoon
téré dar pe a'ke sada karoon
tujhé ghamgusār ki ho talab t'o teré
    huzoor méin ā'rahoon
yé na ho t'o soo-é rah-é adam main
    phir ek bar ravanah hoon

A Wish

I have no fath in miracles
but this wish I do nurture
that when death carries me away from the world,
it should grant me this permission, just once
that I may return from the grave
and, knocking at your door, cry out
if you need a consoler
I'm here.
And if you don't need one,
I may return again to the other world.

Sāl-gi'rah

سالگرہ

Sha'ir ka jashn-é-sāl-gi'rah hai,
   sharāb la
mansab, <u>kh</u>itab, rutba unhein kya
   nahin mila
bas nuqs hai t'o itna ké mamdooh
   ne koi
misr'a kisi kitab ké shayān nahin
   likha

شاعر کا جشنِ سالگرہ ہے، شراب لا
منصب، خطاب، رتبہ انہیں کیا نہیں ملا
بس نقص ہے تو اتنا کہ ممدوح نے کوئی
مصرع کسی کتاب کے شایاں نہیں لکھا

Anniversary

Bring up some wine, it's a poet's anniversary!
What has not come his way--office, title, status.
There's just this snag though, that the one eulogized
never wrote a single line worthy of any book.

Din Aur rāt

دن اور رات

Tīr'agī jāl hai aur bhala hai noor

ek shikari hai din, ek shikari hai
rāt

jag samandar hai jis mein kinare se
doōr

machliyon ki tar'h ibn-e-adam ki
zāt

jag samandar hai, sāhil pe hain
māhi' gīr

jāl thāme koi, koi bhāla liye

meri bari kab a'egi kya janiye

din ke bhāle se mujh ko karein ge
shikar

rāt ke jāl mein ya karein ge aseer?

تیرگی جال ہے اور بھالا ہے نور

اک شکاری ہے دن، اک شکاری ہے رات

جگ سمندر ہے، جس میں کنارے سے دور

مچھلیوں کی طرح ابنِ آدم کی ذات

جگ سمندر ہے، ساحل پہ ہیں ماہی گیر

جال تھامے کوئی، کوئی بھالا لئے

میری باری کب آئے گی کیا جانئے

دن کے بھالے سے مجھ کو کریں گے شکار

رات کے جال میں یا کریں گے اسیر؟

Day and Night

Darkness a net, and light a spear;
day a hunter, and so is the night.
This world is a sea in which, far from the shore,
live Adam's progeny, like the fish.
The world is a sea on whose shore stand
                                        the fishermen;
some holding nets, others spears.
Who knows when my turn will come
to be hunted down by the day's spear,
or be caught in the night's net.

Ham ne sab sher mein sanvare thay
ham se jitne sukhan tumhare thay

هم نے سب شعر میں سنوارے تھے
ہم سے جتنے سخن تمہارے تھے

Rang-o-khushboo ke husn-o-khoobi
ke
tum se thay jitne ist'āre thay
tere qaul-o-qarar se paihle
apne kuch aur bhi sahare thay

رنگ و خوشبو کے حسن و خوبی کے
تم سے تھے جتنے استعارے تھے

تیرے قول و قرار سے پہلے
اپنے کچھ اور بھی سہارے تھے

jab voh lal-o-gohar hisab kiye
jo tere gham ne dil pe va're thay
mere daman mein ā'gire sa're
jitne tasht-e falak mein ta're thay
um'r-e- javed ki du'a karte
Faiz itne voh kab hamare thay

جب وہ لعل و گہر حساب کئے
جو تیرے غم نے دل پہ وارے تھے
میرے دامن میں آگرے سارے
جتنے طشت فلک میں تارے تھے
عمر جاوید کی دعا کرتے
فیض اتنے وہ کب ہمارے تھے

All That You Ever Said to Me

All that you ever said to me
embellished my verse;
all my metaphors were a gift from you--
of colour and fragrance, of beauty and grace.

Indeed,there were other props too for my life,
before your pledges and promises,

while counting all those gems and rubies
your sorrow had bestowed on my heart,

all the stars from the sky's platter
fell into my lap.

Oh, to pray for my eternal life--
when, O Faiz, was she ever so much mine?

Méré dard ko jo zabān mi'lé

مرے درد کو جو زباں ملے

Méra dard naghma-é be sada

مرا درد نغمہ ٔ بے صدا

méri zāt zarra-é be-nishań

مری ذات ذرہ ٔ بے نشاں

méré dard ko jo zaban mi'lé

مرے درد کو جو زباں ملے

mujhé apna nam-o nishan mi'lé

مجھے اپنا نام و نشاں ملے

méri zāt ka jo nishan mi'lé

مری ذات کا جو نشاں ملے

mujhé rāz-é-nazm-e jahan mi'lé

مجھے رازِ نظم جہاں ملے

jo mujhé yé rāz-é-nihan mi'lé

جو مجھے یہ رازِ نہاں ملے

méri khamushi ko bayān milé

مری خامشی کو بیاں ملے

Mujhé ka'inat ki sarwari

مجھے کائنات کی سروری

mujhé dault-é-do'jahan mi'lé

مجھے دولتِ دو جہاں ملے

Qat'a

قطعہ

Hazār dard shab-é-arzoo ki rāh mein
   hai

ہزار درد شب آرزو کی راہ میں ہے

koi thikanah bata'o ké qāfilah utré

کوئی ٹھکانہ بتاؤ کہ قافلہ اترے

qarib aur bhi a'o ké shauq-é did mi'té

قریب اور بھی آؤ کہ شوق دید مٹے

sharāb aur pila'o ké kuch nasha'h utré

شراب اور پلاؤ کہ کچھ نشہ اترے

If Pain Could Speak

My pain, a voiceless song,
my being a nameless mote.
If only my pain could speak,
I'd know who I am.
And if my self could find its essence,
I'd unravel the mystery of this world.
If I could seize this hiden mystery,
my silence would find expression.
Then would I lord it over the universe,
possess all treasures of the two worlds.

Quatrain

A thousand aches in the pathway of the
night of desire.
Show me some shelter so the caravan may
come to rest.
Come closer still to me so that my eager eyes
may be satiated.
Bring me some wine, more wine, so that my
intoxication may wear off.

Pā'on sé lahoo ko dho'dālo

پاؤں سے لہو کو دھو ڈالو

ہم کیا کرتے کس رہ چلتے

Ham kya karté kis rah chalté
har rāh mein kānté bikhré thay
u'n rishton ko jo choot ga'é
u'n sadyon ke yāranon ké
jo ek ek kar'ké toot ga'é
jis rāh cha'le, jis simt ga'é
yoon paon lahoo-lahan hu'é

ہر راہ میں کانٹے بکھرے تھے
ان رشتوں کے جو چھوٹ گئے
ان صدیوں کے یاروں کے
جو اک اک کر کے ٹوٹ گئے
جس راہ چلے، جس سمت گئے
یوں پاؤں لہو لہان ہوئے

Sab dékhne vā'lé kaihte thay
yé kaisi rīt racha'i hai
yé mehndi kyo'on laga'i hai
voh kaihte thay, kyoon qaih't-é vafa
ka nā'haq charchah karté ho
pa'on se lahoo ko dho'dalo!
yé rahein jab a't ja'éngi
sau raste u'n sé phootein'gé
tum dil ko sambhalo jis mein abhi
sau tar'h ké nashtar tootein'gé

سب دیکھنے والے کہتے تھے
یہ کیسی ریت رچائی ہے
یہ مہندی کیوں لگائی ہے
وہ کہتے تھے، کیوں قطع وفا
کا ناحق چرچا کرتے ہو
پاؤں سے لہو کو دھو ڈالو!
یہ راہیں جب اٹ جائیں گی
سورتے ان سے پھوٹیں گے
تم دل کو سنبھالو جس میں ابھی
سو طرح کے نشتر ٹوٹیں گے

159

Wash the Blood Off Your Feet

What could we do--where could we go?
Thorns were strewn on every pathway.
Those bonds, now sundered--
those friendships of centuries
broken, one by one;
whichever way we went, in whatever direction,
the feet were bathed in blood.

Said all those who saw:
what rite is this,
why these hennaed feet?
Said they:why this futile talk
about the drought of loyalty?

Wash the blood off your feet!
When these pathways will be closed,
a hundred new routes will branch out.
You'd better hold your heart
in which a hundred different lancets will break.

A'i shām meh'rbān ho!

اے شام مہرباں ہو!

A'i sham méh'rbān ho
اے شام مہرباں ہو

a'i sham-é shaihr-é yāran
اے شام شہریاراں

ham pé meh'rban ho
ہم پہ مہرباں ہو

dozakhi d'o paihr sitam ki
دوزخی دو پہر ستم کی

bé'sabab sitam ki
بے سبب ستم کی

d'o paihr dard-o-ghaiz-o-gham ki
دو پہر درد و غیظ و غم کی

bé zaban dard-o-ghaiz-o-gham ki
بے زباں درد و غیض و غم کی

i's dozakhi d'o paihr ke taziya'né
اس دوزخی دو پہر کے تازیانے

āj tan par dhanak ki soorat
آج تن پر دھنک کی صورت

khaus dar khaus b'at ga'é hain
قوس در قوس بٹ گئے ہیں

zakhm sab khul ga'é hain
زخم سب کھل گئے ہیں

dāgh jana tha ch'at ga'é hain
داغ جانا تھا چھپ گئے ہیں

téré t'oshe mein kuch t'o ho'ga
ترے توشے میں کچھ تو ہوگا

marham-é-dard ka d'oshala
مرہم درد کا دوشالہ

tan ke u's ang par urha'dé
تن کے اس انگ پر اڑھا دے

dard sab se siva jahān ho
درد سب سے سوا جہاں ہو

a'i sham meh'rban ho
اے شام مہرباں ہو

a'i sham-é-shaihr-é yarān
اے شام شہریاراں

ham pé meh'rban ho
ہم پہ مہرباں ہو

d'ozakhi dasht nafrat'on ke
دوزخی دشت نفرتوں کے

be-dard nafrat'on ke
بے درد نفرتوں کے

kirchian didah-é-hasad ki
کرچیاں دیدۂ حسد کی

(khas-o-khāshāk ranjish'on ke)
(خس و خاشاک رنجشوں کے)

Evening, Be Gracious

O evening, be gracious--
O evening of the city of friends
be gracious to me.
The hellish noon of oppression,
senseless cruelties,
the noon of pain, rage and sorrow,
inarticulate pain, rage and sorrow,
the whiplashes of this demonic noon--
are all, like the rainbow, branded on my body,
arc within arc.

I thought the scars had vanished
but now even the wounds have come alive.
Surely, there must be something
in your sack--a shawl
to cover up that part of the body
where the pain is most intense.
O evening, be gracious--
O evening of the city of friends,
be gracious to me.

The infernal wilderness of scorn,
callous scorn--
splinters of jealous eyes--

itni sūn'sān shāhrahein,

اتنی سنسان شاہراہیں،

itni gūnjān qat'l gahein

اتنی گنجان قتل گاہیں

jin se ā'e'hain ham guzar kar

جن سے آئے ہیں ہم گزر کر

ā'blah ban ke har qadam par

آبلہ بن کے ہر قدم پر

yoon pa'on kat ga'e'hain

یوں پاؤں کٹ گئے ہیں

raste simat ga'e'hain

رستے سمٹ گئے ہیں

makhmalein apne badalon ki

مخملیں اپنے بادلوں کی

āj pa'on ta'le bicha'de

آج پاؤں تلے بچھادے

shāfi-e-karb-e rahravān ho

شافی کرب رہرواں ہو

a'i shām méh'rban ho

اے شام مہرباں ہو

a'i māh-e-shab nigaran

اے مہ شب نگاراں

a'i rafiq-e dil'figaran

اے رفیق وافگاراں

i's sham hamzaban ho

اس شام ہمزباں ہو

a'i sham méh'rban ho

اے شام مہرباں ہو

a'i sham méh'rban ho

اے شام مہرباں ہو

a'i shām-e-shaihr-e yarān

اے شامِ شہریاراں

ham pé méh'rban ho

ہم پہ مہرباں ہو

the litter of estrangement.
Such dreary highways,
so many crowded abbatoirs,
through which we have passed,
like blisters at every step.
This is how our feet have been bruised,
pathways have shrunken.
Spread out today your velvety clouds
under our feet;
be the alleviator of suffering wayfarers.

O evening, be gracious.
O moon of the night of love,
O consoler of agonized hearts
commune with us this evening.
O evening, be gracious;
O evening of the city of friends,
be gracious to us.

Kuch ishq kiya, kuch kām kiya

کچھ عشق کیا، کچھ کام کیا

voh lo'g bahut khush qismat thay

jo ishq ko kām samajhte thay

ya kām se āshiqi karte thay

ham ji'té ji masroof rahé

kuch ishq kiya, kuch kām kiya

kām ishq ke ā'ṛé ā'tā rahā

aur ishq se kam ulajhta raha

phir ā'khir tang akar ham né

donon ko adhoora choṛ diya

وہ لوگ بہت خوش قسمت تھے

جو عشق کو کام سمجھتے تھے

یا کام سے عاشقی کرتے تھے

ہم جیتے جی مصروف رہے

کچھ عشق کیا، کچھ کام کیا،

کام عشق کے آڑے آتا رہا

اور عشق سے کام الجھتا رہا

پھر آخر تنگ آکر ہم نے

دونوں کو ادھورا چھوڑ دیا

Some Love, Some Work

Fortunate indeed were those
who took love as their business
or were in love with whatever they did.
I remained busy all my life--
some love, some work.

Work came in the way of love
and love often impeded work.

Then, finally, in disgust, giving it all up,
I forsook them both, half done.

Dil-é-ma'n musafir-é-ma'n

دلِ من مسافرِ من

Mére dil, mére musafir

hū'a phir se hukm sādir

ke vatan badar hon ham tum

dein gali gali sada'ein

karein rukh nagar nagar ka

ké surāgh koi pa'ein

kisi yār-é nama'bar ka

har ek ajnabi se poochein

jo pata tha apné ghar ka

sar-é koo'-é nashnayān

hamein din sé rāt karna

kabhi i's sé bāt karna

kabhi u's sé bāt karna

tumhein kya kahoon ké kya hai

shab-é gham būri bala hai

hamein yé bhi tha ghanimat

jo koi shumar hota

hamein kya būra tha marna

agar ek bār ho'ta!

مرے دل، مرے مسافر

ہوا پھر سے حکم صادر

کہ وطن بدر ہوں ہم تم

دیں گلی گلی صدائیں

کریں رخ نگر نگر کا

کہ سراغ کوئی پائیں

کسی یار نامہ بر کا

ہر اک اجنبی سے پوچھیں

جو پتا تھا اپنے گھر کا

سر کوئے ناشنایاں

ہمیں دن سے رات کرنا

کبھی اس سے بات کرنا

کبھی اس سے بات کرنا

تمہیں کیا کہوں کہ کیا ہے

شبِ غم بری بلا ہے

ہمیں یہ بھی تھا غنیمت

جو کوئی شمار ہو تا

ہمیں کیا برا تھا مرنا

اگر ایک بار ہو تا!

167

My Heart, My Fellow Traveller

O my heart, my fellow-traveller,
once again it's decreed
that we should both be exiled,
let our wailings resound down every lane,
wend our way from town to town
to pick up some friend
with a message from the beloved.

We shall ask every stranger
about our last dwelling.

Standing at the head of some lane where strangers live,
as the day will pass into night,
I'll hold in talk
sometimes this one, sometimes that one.

How shall I tell you
what a curse the night of separation is !
Even dying would be endurable
if one could keep count
of the myriad deaths.

Death would not have mattered to us at all
if it would strike only once!

Āj ek harf ko phir dhoondta phirta hai khayal

آج اِک حرف کو پھر ڈھونڈتا پھرتا ہے خیال

Āj ek harf ko phir dhoondta phirta
hai khayal

madh bhara harf koi, zaih'r bhara harf
koi

dil nashin harf koi, qaih'r bhara harf
koi

harf-é ulfat koi dildar nazar ho jaisé

jis sé milti hai nazar bo'sah'-é lab ki
soorat

itna raushan ké sar-é mauja-é zar ho
jaisé

sohbat-é-yār mein āghāz-é-tarab ki
soorat

harf-é-nafrat koi shamshīr-é ghazab
ho jaisé

tā abad shaih'r-é-sitam jis sé taba'h ho
jā'éin

itna tarīk ké shamshan ki shab ho
jaisé

lab pé lā'oon t'o mere ho'nt siyah ho
jā'éin

آج اِک حرف کو پھر ڈھونڈ تا پھر تا ہے خیال

مدھ بھرا حرف کوئی، زہر بھرا حرف کوئی

دل نشیں حرف کوئی، قہر بھرا حرف کوئی

حرفِ الفت کوئی دلدار نظر ہو جیسے

جس سے ملتی ہے نظر بوسۂ لب کی صورت

اتنا روشن کہ سرِ موجۂ زر ہو جیسے

صحبتِ یار میں آغازِ طرب کی صورت

حرفِ نفرت کوئی شمشیرِ غضب ہو جیسے

تابہ ابد شہرِ ستم جس سے تہہ ہو جائیں

اتنا تاریک کہ شمشان کی شب ہو جیسے

لب پہ لاؤں تو مرے ہونٹ سیہ ہو جائیں

Today Again is Imagination Seeking a Word

Today again is imagination seeking a word--
some word sweet, or a word soaked in venom.
A word alluring, a word dreadful;
a word of love, enthralling as love's glance
which my eye meets, like the meeting of lips--
effulgent like the crest of a wave of gold.
A word like a prelude to merriment in the
                         beloved's company,
or a word of hate, like an angry sword
that could destroy all the cities of oppression,
                         till eternity--
a word as dark as the night in a crematorium,
so dark that if uttered it may blacken the lips.

Phool murjha ga'e sāre

پھول مرجھا گئے سارے

Phool murjha ga'e sāre

thamt'e nahin hain āsman ke ānsoo

sham'ein be-noor ho'gai hain

ā'ine choor ho ga'e hain

sāz sab baj ke kho ga'e hain

payal'ein bujh ke so'ga'i hain

aur in badalon ke piche

door i's rāt ka dulara

پھول مرجھا گئے سارے

تھمتے نہیں ہیں آسماں کے آنسو

شمعیں بے نور ہو گئی ہیں

آئینے چور ہو گئے ہیں

ساز سب بج کے کھو گئے ہیں

پایلیں بجھ کے سو گئی ہیں

اوران بادلوں کے پیچھے

دور اس رات کا دلارا

dard ka sitara

timtima raha hai

jhunjhuna raha hai

muskura raha hai

درد کا ستارا

ٹمٹما رہا ہے

جھنجھنا رہا ہے

مسکرا رہا ہے

All the Flowers Have Withered Away

All the flowers have withered away.
No let up in the flow of the sky's tears.
The lamps have gone lustreless,
the mirrors lie shattered,
and all the orchestras have played
                                    themselves out.
The ankle-bells have done their jingling
and behind the clouds,
far away, this night's beloved,
the star of pain
is twinkling
tinkling
smiling.

Koi āshiq kisi mahbooba'h sé

کوئی عاشق کسی محبوبہ سے

گلشن یاد میں گر آج دم باد صبا

Gulsha'n-é-yād mein gar āj dam'-é
bād-é-saba

پھر سے چاہے کہ گل افشاں ہو تو ہو جانے دو

Phir se cha'hé ke gul'afshan ho t'o
ho' jāné d'o

عمر رفتہ کے کسی طاق پہ بسرا ہوا درد

Um'r-é rafta ké kisi tāq pé bisra
hu'ā dard

پھر سے چاہے کہ فروزاں ہو تو ہو جانے دو

phir sé chāh'e ké farozaṅ ho t'o ho
ja'né d'o

جیسے بیگانہ سے اب ملتے ہو ویسے ہی سہی

Jaisé be'gāna'h sé ab mil'té ho
vaisé hi sa'hi

آؤ دو چار گھڑی میرے مقابل بیٹھو

Ā'o d'o chār ghaṛi méré muqabil
bai'tho

گرچہ مل بیٹھیں گے ہم تم تو ملاقات کے بعد

garché'h mil baithein'gé ham tum
t'o mulaqāt ke bā'd

اپنا احساس زیاں اور زیادہ ہو گا

apna ehsas-é-ziyaṅ aur ziyadah
ho'ga

ہم سخن ہوں گے جو ہم دونوں تو ہر بات کے بیچ

ham sukhan ho'ngé j'o ham
dono'n t'o har bāt ké bīch

ان کہی بات کا موہوم سا پردہ ہو گا

a'n kahi bāt ka mauhoom sa
pardah hoga

کوئی اقرار میں یاد دلاؤں گا نہ تم

koi iqrār na mai'n yād dila'on ga
na tum

کوئی مضمون وفا کا نہ جفا کا ہو گا

koi mazmoon vafa ka na jafa ka
hoga

گرد ایام کی تحریر کو دھونے کے لئے

gard-é-ayyam ki tahrir ko dho'ne
ke liyé

تم سے گویا ہوں دم دید جو میری پلکیں

tum se go'ya ho'n dam-é d'id j'o
méri palkein

تم جو چاہو تو سنو، اور جو نہ چاہو نہ سنو

tum j'o cha'ho t'o su'no, aur j'o na
cha'ho na su'no

اور جو حرف کریں مجھ سے گریزاں آنکھیں

aur j'o harf karéin mujh sé gurézaṅ
ankhéin

تم جو چاہو ہو تو کہو، اور جو نہ چاہو نہ کہو

tum j'o cha'ho t'o kaho, aur j'o na
cha'ho na kaho.

Some Lover to His Beloved

If in memory's garden today, the breeze blows
                              this moment,
again longing to scatter flowers, then let it be.
If in the niche of days gone by, some forgotten pain
again yearns to be rekindled, then let it be.
Let it be as you'd meet a stranger--
come, just sit there in front of me for a while.
If we'd get together, you and me, then
our sense of loss will grow still more intense;
if we'd lend ourselves to a little talk; between words
there'll hang a fine screen of things left unsaid.
Neither will I remind you of any vow, nor you--
there'll be not a word about commitment
                              or callousness.

To wipe out the writing of time's dust,
if my eyes speak when I glance at you,
you may listen if you like, or not if you don't.
And if your evasive eyes choose to censure me,
you may say anything you like, or nothing
                              if you don't.

Shā'ir Lo'g

شاعر لوگ

Har ek daur méin ham, har
    zamané méin ham
zaih'r pi'té rah'é, gīt gāt'e rah'é
jān dé'té rah'é zindagi ke liyé
sā'at-é-vas'l ki sarkhushi ke liyé

dīn-o-dunya ki daulat luta'té
    ra'hé,
faq'r-o-faqa'h ka to'sha
    sambha'lé hu'é
J'o bhi rasta chuna u's pé
    chal'té rah'é
māl vā'lé hiqarat sé tak'té rah'é
ta'n karté rah'é, hāth mal'té
    rah'é
Ham né u'n par kiya harf-e-haq
    sa'ng za'n
Jin ki haibat se dunya larazti
    rahi
Jin pe ānsoo ba'hāné ko koi na
    tha
apni ānkh u'n ke gham mein
    barasti rahi
sab se aujhal hu'é hukm-e
    hākim pé ham
qaid khan'é sahé, tazia'né sa'hé
Lo'g sun'té rahé sāz-e-dil ki
    sada
apné naghmé salakh'on sé
    chan'té rah'é
Khoon'chakān daih'r ká
    khoon'chakan ā'inah
dukh bhari khálq ka dukh
    bhara dil hain ham
tab'é sha'ir hai jangah-é-
    adl-o-sitam
munsif-e-khair-o-shar
    haq-o-batil hain ham.

ہر اک دور میں ہم، ہر زمانے میں ہم

زہر پیتے رہے، گیت گاتے رہے

جان دیتے رہے زندگی کے لئے

ساعتِ وصل کی سر خوشی کے لئے

دین و دنیا کی دولت لٹاتے رہے

فقر و فاقہ کا توشہ سنبھالے ہوئے

جو بھی رستہ چنا اس پہ چلتے رہے

مال والے حقارت سے تکتے رہے

طعن کرتے رہے، ہاتھ ملتے رہے

ہم نے ان پر کیا حرف حق سنگ زن

جن کی ہیبت سے دنیا لرزتی رہی

جن پہ آنسو بہانے کو کوئی نہ تھا

اپنی آنکھ ان کے غم میں برستی رہی

سب سے اوجھل ہوئے حکم حاکم پہ ہم

قیدِ خانے سہے، تازیانے سہے

لوگ سنتے رہے سازِ دل کی صدا

اپنے نغمے سلاخوں سے چھنتے رہے

خوں چکاں دہر کا خوں چکاں آئینہ

دکھ بھری خلق کا دکھ بھرا دل ہیں ہم

طبع شاعر ہے جنگاہ عدل و ستم

منصفِ خیر و شر، حق و باطل ہیں ہم

We Poets

We were there-- in every age, in every clime,
drinking poison, singing songs;
we kept sacrificing ourselves for life's sake--
for the moment of rapture at love's union.
We kept squandering away our treasure of
                                spirit and matter,
holding on to our provision of deprivation and hunger.
Whatever path we chose, we stuck to it
even while the affluent kept staring at us disdainfully,
reproachfully, rubbing their palms.
On them we hurled the stone of the word of truth
whose dread kept the world reeling.
And for those who'd none to shed tears over,
our eyes rained tears for their sorrow.
At the ruler's command, we went out of sight,
endured prisons, suffered flogging.
As people listened to the strains of our hearts' cries,
our songs kept filtering through the prison bars.
We are the blood-stained mirrors of this
                                blood-stained world,
we are the sorrowful heart of anguished humankind.
A poet's temper is to battle against injustice and
                                tyranny;
we are the arbiters of good and evil, right and wrong.

Ye mātam-e vaqt ki ghari hai

یہ ماتم وقت کی گھڑی ہے

thaih'r ga'i āsman ki nad'ya

voh ja lagi hai ufaq kina're

udas rangon ki chand nai'ya

utar ga'e sahil-e-zamin par
sabhi khivai'ya

tamām ta're

ukhar ga'i sāns pattiyon ki

chali ga'in oongh mein hava'ein

gajar baja hukm-e khāmushi ka

t'o chup mein gūm hoga'in sada'ein

sahar ki gori ki chatiyon se

dhalak ga'i tīragi ki chadar

aur i's baja'e

bikhar ga'e u's ke tan badan par

nirās tanhāiyon ke sā'e

aur u's ko kuch bhi khabar nahin hai

kisi ko kuch bhi khabar nahin hai

ke din dha'le shaih'r se nikal kar

kidhar ko ja'ne ka rukh kiya tha

na koi jāda'h, na koi manzil

kisi musafir ko

ab damāgh-e-safar nahin hai

ye vaqt zanjir-e roz-o-shab ki

kahin se tooti hu'i kari hai

ye mātam-e-vaqt ki ghari hai

تھہر گئی آساں کی ندیا

وہ جا لگی ہے افق کنارے

اداس رنگوں کی چاند نیا

اتر گئے ساحل زمیں پر

سبھی کھویا

تمام تارے

اکھڑ گئی سانس پتیوں کی

چلی گئی اودھ میں ہوائیں

گجر بجا حکم خامشی کا

تو چپ میں گم ہو گئیں صدائیں

سحر کی گوری کی چھاتیوں سے

ڈھلک گئی تیرگی کی چادر

اور اس بجائے

بکھر گئے اس کے تن بدن پر

نراس تنہائیوں کے سائے

اور اس کو کچھ بھی خبر نہیں ہے

کسی کو کچھ بھی خبر نہیں ہے

کہ دن ڈھلے شہر سے نکل کر

کدھر کو جانے کا رخ کیا تھا

نہ کوئی جادہ، نہ کوئی منزل

کسی مسافر کو

اب دماغ سفر نہیں ہے

یہ وقت زنجیر روزوشب کی

کہیں سے ٹوٹی ہوئی کڑی ہے

یہ ماتم وقت کی گھڑی ہے

This is the Moment to Mourn Time

The sky's stream has come to a standstill.
There, the moon's dismal coloured boat
has reached the horizon's fringe.
All the boatmen, all the stars,
have landed on the earth's shore--
The leaves are panting for breath,
the winds have dozed off.
At daybreak, as silence was decreed,
all sounds faded away.
From the breasts of the fair damsel of dawn
has slipped off the shawl of darkness
and instead
are now scattered all over her body-
the shadows of desolate loneliness.
Neither does the dawn know,
nor anybody else, where
at dusk he's set out to go,
leaving the city.
No pathway, no destination;
no traveller has now any inclination for journeying.
This moment, the chain of day and night
seems broken at some point.
This is the moment to mourn time.

Yé vaqt ā'é t'o be -irad'ah   یہ وقت آۓ تو بے ارادہ

kabhi kabhi main bhi dékhta hoon   کبھی کبھی میں بھی دیکھتا ہوں

utār kar zāt ka libadah   اتار کر ذات کالبادہ

kahin siyahi malamat'oṅ ki   کہیں سیاہی ملامتوں کی

kahin pé gul'booté ulfat'oṅ ké   کہیں یہ گل بوٹے الفتوں کے

kahin lakiréin hain ānsu'oṅ ki   کہیں لکیریں ہیں آنسوؤں کی

kahin pé khoon-é-jigar ké dhab'bé   کہیں یہ خون جگر کے دھبے

yé chāk hai panjah-é a'doo ka   یہ چاک ہے پنجہ عدو کا

yé meh'r hai yār-é méh'rban ki   یہ مہر ہے یار مہرباں کی

yé la'l lab hā'é mahvash'an ke   یہ لعل لب ہاۓ مہوشاں کے

yé marhamat shaikh-é ba'd zaban ki   یہ مرحمت شیخ بدزباں کی

yé jāma-e roz-o-shab -gazida   یہ جامہ روزوشب گزیدہ

mujhé yé pairahan-é daridah   مجھے یہ پیراہن دریدہ

aziz bhi, na' pasand bhi hai   عزیز بھی، ناپسند بھی ہے

kabhi yé farman-é josh-e-vaihshat   کبھی یہ فرمان جوش و حشت

ke no'ch kar i's ko phaink dalo   کہ نوچ کر اس کو پھینک ڈالو

kabhi yé isrār-e harf-é-ulfat   کبھی یہ اصرار حرف الفت

ke choom kar phir gal'é laga lo   کہ چوم کر پھر گلے لگالو

Whenever this moment arrives, I too,
unwittingly, sometimes see,
taking off the garments of self,
somewhere the stains of reproach,
somewhere love's floral embroidery,
somewhere streaks of tears, and
the blots of heart's blood.
Here broke the enemy's claw,
this is the seal of a loving friend,
these the ruddy lips of gracious beloveds,
this the gift of the foul-mouthed priest.

This tattered robe of day and night,
is to me both dear and disdained.
Sometimes, at the behest of frenzy,
I feel like tearing it to shreds
and at times, at love's insistence,
I want to kiss it,
embrace it again.

Ham t'o majboor-é-vafa hain

ہم تو مجبور و فا ہیں

تجھ کو کتنوں کا لہو چاہیے اے ارض وطن
جو ترے عارض بے رنگ کو گلنار کریں
کتنی آہوں سے کلیجہ ترا ٹھنڈا ہوگا
کتنے آنسو ترے صحراؤں کو گلزار کریں

تیرے ایوانوں میں پرزے ہوئے پیماں کتنے
کتنے وعدے جو نہ آسودۂ اقرار ہوئے
کتنی آنکھوں کو نظر کھا گئی بدخواہوں کی
خواب کتنے تری شہ راہوں میں سنگسار ہوئے

بلا کشان محبت پہ جو ہوا سو ہوا
جو مجھ پہ گزری مت اس سے کہو، ہوا سو ہوا
مبادا ہو کوئی ظالم ترا گریباں گیر
لہو کے داغ تو دامن سے دھو، ہوا سو ہوا

ہم تو مجبور و فا ہیں مگر اے جان جہاں
اپنے عشاق سے ایسے بھی کوئی کرتا ہے
تیری محفل کو خدا رکھے ابد تک قائم
ہم تو مہماں ہیں گھڑی بھر کے ہمارا کیا ہے

tujh ko kitnon ka lahoo chahiye ai
    arz-é-vatan
jo teré āriz-é be' rang ko gulnar karéin
kitni āho'n sé kalijah téra thanda
    hoga
kitné ānsoo téré sahra'on ko gulzar
    karein

tere aivan'on mein purze hu'é paiman
    kitne
kitné va'dé j'o na āsoodah-é-iqrār hu'é
kitni ankh'on ko nazar kha ga'i ba'd
    khāh'on ki
khāb kitne teri shahrah'on méin
    sāngsār hu'é

bala kashan-é mohabbat pe jo hu'ā s'o
    hu'ā
j'o mujh pe guzri mat u's sé kaho,
    hu'a so hu'a
mabada ho koi zalim téra gireban'gir
lahoo ke dāgh t'o daman sé dho,
    hu'a so hu'a

ham to majboor-é-vafa hain magar a'i
    jān-é-jahan
āpne ushaq sé aise bhi koi karta hai
téri maihfil ko khuda rakhé abad tak
    qa'im
ham t'o mehman hain ghari bhar ke
    hamara kyā hai

We Are Committed to Loyalty

The blood of how many do you need,
                          O my motherland,
so that your lustreless cheek may turn crimson?
How many sighs will soothe your heart
--and how many tears make your deserts bloom?

How many pledges lie splintered down your hallways
and how many promises that were never honoured?
How many eyes were cursed by the evil eye
and how many dreams were stoned to death
                          on your highways?

It matters little what suffering was the lot of love--
don't tell her how much I endured--it's all over now.
Lest some tyrant hold you by the scruff,
let the blood be washed off your hem--
what's done is done.

We're indeed committed to loyalty but, O my love,
should lovers be treated so coldly?
Let God keep your assembly going till eternity----
we're only guests for a moment, we don't
                          really matter.

Paris

پیرس

Din dhala, koocha o bazar méin
    saf-basta ho'in

zard roo raushniyan

in méin har ék ké kashkol sé
    barséin rim jhim

i's bhar'e shaihr ki nasoodgiyan

dōor pas'manzar-é-aflāk mein
    dhundla'ne lagé

azmat-é-rafta ke nishan

pésh manzar méin

kisi saya-é-dīvār se lipta hu'ā
    saya'h koi

dōosre sā'é ki mauhoom si ummid
    liyé

roz marrah ki tar'h

zér-é-lab

shar'h-é bedardi-é ayyam ki
    tamhīd liyé

aur koi ajnabi

in raushniyon sayon sé katrata
    hu'a

apné bekhab shabistan ki taraf jata

    hu'a

دن ڈھلا، کوچہ و بازار میں صف بستہ ہوئیں

زرد رو روشنیاں

ان میں ہر ایک کے کشکول سے برسیں رم جھم

اس بھرے شہر کی ناآسودگیاں

دور پس منظر افلاک میں دھند لانے لگے

عظمتِ رفتہ کے نشاں

پیش منظر میں

کسی سایۂ دیوار سے لپٹا ہوا سایہ کوئی

دوسرے سائے کی موہوم سی امید لئے

روز مرہ کی طرح

زیرِ لب

شرح بے دردی ایام کی تمہید لئے

اور کوئی اجنبی

ان روشنیوں سایوں سے کتراتا ہوا

اپنے بے خواب شبستاں کی طرف جاتا ہوا

Paris

The day faded away, and down the streets
                                    and alleyways
were arrayed pallid lampposts
from whose bowls rained down
this crowded city's frustrations.
Over there
the vestiges of past glory
began to look hazy against the skyline
and there, in front of the eye,
some shadow embraced a wall's shadow
cherishing the faint hope for another shadow--
an everyday occurrence--
prefaces a mute comment
on the harshness of time-
and some stranger
skirting these lights, these shadows,
presses on towards his dreamless bed-chamber.

کیا کریں

Kya Karein

مری تری نگاہ میں

Méri téri nigāh méin

جو لاکھ انتظار ہیں

J'o lakh intezar hain

جو میرے تیرے تن بدن میں

J'o méré téré tan badan méin

لاکھ دل فگار ہیں

lakh dil figar hain

جو میری تیری انگلیوں کی بے حسی سے

j'o méri téri ungliyon ki bé' hisi sé

سب قلم نزار ہیں

sab qalam nazār hain

جو میرے تیرے شہر کی

J'o méré téré shaih'r ki

ہر اک گلی میں

har ék gali méin

میرے تیرے نقش پا کے بے نشاں مزار ہیں

Méré téré naqsh-e pa ke bénishan

جو میری تیری رات کے

mazār hain

ستارے زخم زخم ہیں

J'o méri teri rāt ké

جو میری تیری صبح کے

sitaré zakh'm zakh'm hain

گلاب چاک چاک ہیں

J'o méri'téri sub'h ké

یہ زخم سارے بے دوا

gulab chāk chāk hain

یہ چاک سارے بے رفو

yé zakh'm sāré bé-dava

کسی پہ راکھ چاند کی

ye chāk sāré bé rafoo

کسی پہ اوس کا لہو

kisi pé rākh chānd ki

یہ ہے بھی یا نہیں، بتا

kisi pé oas ka lahoo

یہ ہے کہ محض جال ہے

yé hai bhi ya nahin, ba'ta

مرے تمہارے عنکبوت وہم کا بنا ہوا

yé hai ké maih'z jāl hai

جو ہے تو اس کا کیا کریں

méré tumharé ankaboot-é-é-vaih'm ka

نہیں ہے تو بھی کیا کریں

buna hu'a

بتا، بتا

j'o hai to i's ka kya karéin

بتا، بتا

nahin hai t'o bhi kya karéin

ba'ta, ba'ta

ba'ta, ba'ta

What Shall We Do?

In your eyes and mine
endless expectations--
in your body and mine
those countless broken hearts--
all the pens paralyzed
due to numbness
of your fingers and mine.
Anonymous graves of your footprints and mine
in every lane
of your city and mine.
Those stars wounded, of your night and mine,
those roses ripped apart
of your morning and mine--
these are all wounds beyond healing,
these are tears beyond darning.
On some there's the moon's dust,
on others the dew is wasted.
Whether it is, or isn't, you tell me!
Or is it all a mere web
woven by the spiders of my illusion and yours?
If it is--then what shall we do about it?
And if it isn't, even then what's to be done?
Tell me, tell me!

apné in'ām-é husn ke badle   اپنے انعام حسن کے بدلے

ham téhi damanon sé kya léna   ہم تہی دامنوں سے کیا لینا

āj furqat' zadon pé lutf karo   آج فرقت زدوں پہ لطف کرو

phir kabhi sab'r āzma léna   پھر کبھی صبر آز مالینا

Dhalti hai mauj-é-mai ki tar'h rāt in
    dinon   ڈھلتی ہے موج مے کی طرح رات ان دنوں

khilti hai sub'h gul ki tar'h rang o
    boo sé pur   کھلتی ہے صبح گل کی طرح رنگ وبو یے پر

virāň hain jām, pās karo kuch   ویراں ہیں جام، پاس کرو کچھ بہار کا

    bahar ka

dil ārzoo sé pur karo ānkhéin lahoo   دل آرزو سے پر کرو آنکھیں لہو سے پر

    sé pur

                          ہم نے دیکھا ہے مے گساروں کو

ham né dékha hai mai-gusaron ko   پی کے اور جی کے آخرش مرتے

pī ké aur jī ké akhirash marté   جو نہیں پیتے موت کو ان سے

J'o nahin pi'té maut ko u'n sé   کس نے دیکھا ہے در گزر کرتے

kis né dékha hai darguzar karté

Quatrains

In recompense for your beauty's largesse
what would you expect of us, the empty-handed?
Why don't you be kind to those afflicted
       by separation?
There'll be another time to test their patience.

These days the night ebbs, like the wine's
       wave receding.
Dawn breaks like a flower exuding colour
       and fragrance.
Empty are the wine-cups; this is no way to welcome
      spring--
let the heart be filled with desire, the eyes with blood.

Indeed, I have known drunkards--
die they must, finally, drinking and revelling.
And those teetotallers--has anyone seen death
pass them by?

Ishq apné mujrimon ko pa'bajulan lé chala

عشق اپنے مجرموں کو پابجو لاں لے چلا

dār ki rassiyon ke gulooband
gardan mein paihne hu'é
gāné vā'lé shab-o-roz gāté rahé
payaléin bér iyon ki bajaté hu'é
nāchne va'lé dhooméin machaté
rahé
ham na i's saf méin thay aur na u's
saf méin thay
rāsté mein khar é un'ko takté rahé
rashk karté rahé
aur chup chap ānsoo bahaté rahé
laut kar ā'ké dékha to phoolon ka
rang
j'o kabhi surkh tha zard hi zard hai
apna paihloo tatola to aisa laga
dil jahan tha vahan dard hi dard
hai
aur guloo méin kabhi tauq ka
vāhéma
kabhi pāo'n mein rakhs zanjir ka
aur phir ék din ishq u'nhin ki tar'h
rasan dar guloo, pabajaulan hamein
u'si qafile méin kashan lé chala

دار کی رسیوں کے گلو بند گردن میں پہنے ہوئے
گانے والے شب و روز گاتے رہے
پا ئلیں بیڑیوں کی بجاتے ہوئے
ناچنے والے دھوم میں مچاتے رہے
ہم نہ اس صف میں تھے اور نہ اس صف میں تھے
راستے میں کھڑے ان کو تکتے رہے
رشک کرتے رہے
اور چپ چاپ آنسو بہاتے رہے
لوٹ کر آکے دیکھا تو پھولوں کا رنگ
جو کبھی سرخ تھا زرد ہی زرد ہے
اپنا پہلو ٹٹولا تو ایسا لگا
دل جہاں تھا وہاں درد ہی درد ہے
اور گلو میں کبھی طوق کا وہم
کبھی پاؤں میں رقص زنجیر کا
اور پھر ایک دن عشق انہیں کی طرح
رسن در گلو، پابجو لاں ہمیں
اسی قافلہ میں کشاں لے چلا

189

Love's Prisoners

Wearing the hangman's noose, like a necklace,
the singers kept on singing day and night,
kept jingling the ankle-bells of their fetters
and the dancers jigged on
riotously.
We who were neither in this camp nor that
just stood by watching them
enviously
shedding silent tears.

Returning, we saw that the crimson
of flowers had turned pale
and on probing within, it seemed
that where the heart once was
now lingered only stabbing pain.
Round our necks the hallucination of a noose,
and on our feet the dance of fetters.

Then came love, one day,
and like the others, enchained, haltered,
we too were dragged into its caravan.

Tum hi kaho kya karna hai

تم ہی کہو کیا کرنا ہے

Jab dukh ki nad'ya méin ham né
jivan ki nā'o dāli thi
tha kitna kas bal banhon méin
lohoo méin kitni lāli thi
yoon lagta tha d'o hath lagé
aur nāo pooram par lagi
aisa na hu'a, har dhāré méin
kuch an'dékhi manjdharéin thīen
kuch manjhi thay anjan bahut
kuch béparkhi patvaréin thien
ab j'o bhi chaho chaan karo
ab jitne chaho dosh dharo
nadya t'o vohi hai nā'o vohi
ab tum hi kaho kya karna hai
ab kaise pār utarna hai
jab apni chāti mein ham ne
i's désh ke ghao dekhé thay
tha vedon par vishvash bahut
aur yad bahut se nuskhé thay
yoon lagta tha bas kuch din méin
sarī bipta kat jā'égi
aur sab ghā'o bharja'ein gé
aisa na hū'a ké rog apné

جب دکھ کی ندیا میں ہم نے
جیون کی ناؤ ڈالی تھی
تھا کتنا کس بل بانہوں میں
لوہو میں کتنی لالی تھی
یوں لگتا تھا دو ہاتھ لگے
اور ناؤ پورم پار لگی
ایسا نہ ہوا، ہر دھارے میں
کچھ ان دیکھی منجدھاریں تھیں
کچھ مانجھی تھے انجان بہت
کچھ بے پرکھی پتواریں تھیں
اب جو بھی چاہو چھان کرو
اب جتنے چاہو دوش دھرو
ندیا تو وہی ہے ناؤ وہی
اب تم ہی کہو کیا کرنا ہے
اب کیسے پار اترنا ہے
جب اپنی چھاتی میں ہم نے
اس دیس کے گھاؤ دیکھے تھے
تھا ویدوں پر وشواش بہت
اور یاد بہت سے نسخے تھے
یوں لگتا تھا بس کچھ دن میں
ساری بپتا کٹ جائے گی
اور سب گھاؤ بھر جائیں گے
ایسا نہ ہوا کہ روگ اپنے

191

What's to be Done, You Tell

When in the river of pain, we
launched the boat of life,
how much vigour there was in our arms
and how red our blood was.
It seemed that just the push of two hands
and the boat would ferry right across.
But this was not to be--in every current
were unseen whirlpools,
then there were some boatmen--utter novices
and there were also some untried oars.
Now it's for you to probe;
now you may lay any blame at our door--
though it's the same river, the same boat.
Now, you tell us what's to be done,
how are we to get across?
When in our bosom we'd seen the wounds
of this land, we had great faith
in our physicians, and remembered
                              many a prescription.
It then seemed as though in just a few days
all our troubles would be over--
all wounds healed.
It wasn't that our ailments
were so chronic, or that our physicians

kuch itné dhér purane thay

vaid u'n ki t'oh ko pa na sa'ke

aur t'onke sab bekar ga'é

ab j'o bhi chāho chān karo

ab jitne chāho dosh dharo

chati t'o vohi hai ghā'o vohi

ab tum hi kaho kya karna hai

ye ghā'o kaisé bharna hai

کچھ اتنے ڈھیر پرانے تھے

وید اُن کی ٹوہ کو پانہ سکے

اور ٹونکے سب بیکار گئے

اب جو بھی چاہو چھان کرو

اب جتنے چاہو دوش دھرو

چھاتی تو وہی ہے گھاؤ وہی

اب تم ہی کہو کیا کرنا ہے

یہ گھاؤ کیسے بھرنا ہے

could not diagnose them--
yet all the curing went in vain.
Now it's for you to probe,
and you may lay all blame at our door.
But it's the same bosom, the same wounds--
now you tell us what's to be done--
how to heal these wounds?

Āj shab koi nahin hai

آج شب کوئی نہیں ہے

Āj shab dil ke qarīn koi nahin hai
ānkh se dōor tilismath ke dar vā
    hain ka'ī
khab dar khab mahallat ke dar va
    hain ka'i
aur makīn koi nahin hai
āj shab dil ke qarin koi nahin hai
"koi naghma, koi khushboo, koi
    kafir soorat"
koi ummid, koi ās musafir soorat
koi gham, koi kasak, koi shak, koi
    yaqin
koi nahin hai
āj shab dil ke qarin koi nahin hai
tum agar ho, t'o mere pās ho ya
    dōor ho tum
har ghaṛi saya gar-é-khatir-é
    ranjoor ho tum
aur nahin ho to kahin--- koi nahin,
    koi nahin hai
āj shab dil ke qarin koi nahin hai

آج شب دل کے قریں کوئی نہیں ہے
آنکھ سے دور طلسمات کے دروابیں کئی
خواب در خواب محلات کے دروابیں کئی
اور مکیں کوئی نہیں ہے،
آج شب دل کے قریں کوئی نہیں ہے
"کوئی نغمہ، کوئی خوشبو، کوئی کافر صورت"
کوئی امید، کوئی آس مسافر صورت
کوئی غم، کوئی کسک، کوئی شک، کوئی یقیں
کوئی نہیں ہے
آج شب دل کے قریں کوئی نہیں ہے
تم اگر ہو، تو مرے پاس ہو یا دور ہو تم
ہر گھڑی سایہ گرِ خاطرِ رنجور ہو تم
اور نہیں ہو تو کہیں۔۔۔ کوئی نہیں، کوئی نہیں ہے
آج شب دل کے قریں کوئی نہیں ہے،

Nobody Around Tonight

There's nobody near my heart tonight.
Far from the eyes are open many magic portals,
several doors to the palaces of dreams within dreams--
but no inmate.
There's nobody near my heart tonight--
no song, no fragrance, no beloved;
hope adrift like a wayfarer--
no sorrow, no ache, no misgiving, no certitide--
nothing whatsoever.

There's nobody near my heart tonight.
If you're there, whether near me or far away,
then every moment you are a solace for the
                                    stricken heart.
And if you're not anywhere, there's nobody
                                    around, no one--
there's nobody near my heart tonight.

I's vaqt t'o yoon lagta hai

اس وقت تو یوں لگتا ہے

I's vaqt t'o yoon lagta hai ab kuch bhi
    nahin hai
mahtab na sooraj, na andhéra na
    savera

اس وقت تو یوں لگتا ہے اب کچھ بھی نہیں ہے
مہتاب نہ سورج، نہ اندھیرا نہ سویرا

ānkhon ke darichon pe kisi husn ki
    chilman
aur dil ki panahon méin kisi dard ka
    dera

آنکھوں کے دریچوں پہ کسی حسن کی چلمن
اور دل کی پناہوں میں کسی درد کا ڈیرا

mumkin hai koi vah'm tha, mumkin
    hai suna ho
galyon méin kisi chāp ka ek akhri
    phéra

ممکن ہے کوئی وہم تھا، ممکن ہے سنا ہو
گلیوں میں کسی چاپ کا اک آخری پھیرا

shakhon mein khayalon ke ghané péŗ
    ki shayad
ab a'ke kare ga na koi khab basera

شاخوں میں خیالوں کے گھنے پیڑ کی شاید
اب آ کے کرے گانہ کوئی خواب بسیرا

ek bair, na ek meh'r, na ek rabt na
    rishta
tera koi apna, na paraya koi méra

اک بیر، نہ اک مہر، نہ اک ربطہ نہ رشتہ
تیرا کوئی اپنا، نہ پرایا کوئی میرا

mana ke yé sunsan ghaŗi sakht kaŗi
    hai
lekin mére dil yé to faqat ek hi ghari
    hai
himmat karo, jīne ko t'o ek umr pari
    hai

مانا کہ یہ سنسان گھڑی سخت کڑی ہے
لیکن مرے دل یہ تو فقط اک ہی گھڑی ہے
ہمت کرو، جینے کو تو اک عمر پڑی ہے

It Seems at This Moment . . .

It seems at this moment nothing exists--
no moon, no sun, neither darkness nor dawn.

In front of the eyes' windows, some beauty behind
                                  the laced curtain
and in the heart's shelter has come to stay some pain.

Perhaps it was some illusoin, or just something
                              I'd heard talked about--
on the street that sound of the last footfalls.

Perhaps in this dense tree, in fancy's boughs,
no dream will ever come to seek refuge.

No estrangement, no affection, no involvement
nobody is yours, for me nobody a stranger.

It's true that this lonesome moment is very cruel
but, O my heart, this is only one such moment.
Take courage, there's all the time to live on.

Tūrk shāi'r Nazim

Hikmat ke afkār

ترک شاعر ناظم حکمت کے افکار

Jīne ke liye marna

ye kaisi sa'ādat hai

mar'né ké liye jīna

ye kaisi himaqat hai

جینے کے لیے مرنا

یہ کیسی سعادت ہے

مرنے کے لیے جینا

یہ کیسی حماقت ہے

akéle jiyo

ek shamshad'tan ki tar'h

aur mil kar jiyo

ek ban ki tar'h

hamne ummid ke sahare par

toot kar yoonhi zindagi kī hai

jis tar'h tum se áshiqi ki hai

اکیلے جیو

ایک شمشاد تن کی طرح

اور مل کر جیو

ایک بن کی طرح

ہم نے امید کے سہارے پر

ٹوٹ کریوں ہی زندگی کی ہے

جس طرح تم سے عاشقی کی ہے

Thoughts of Turkish Poet Nazim Hikmat

To die to live
what good fortune is this.
To live to die
what folly is this.

Walk alone
like an upright box-tree
and live in close togetherness
like the trees in a forest.

Buoyed up on hope,
I've strained my life to its limits -
just as I've been in love with you.